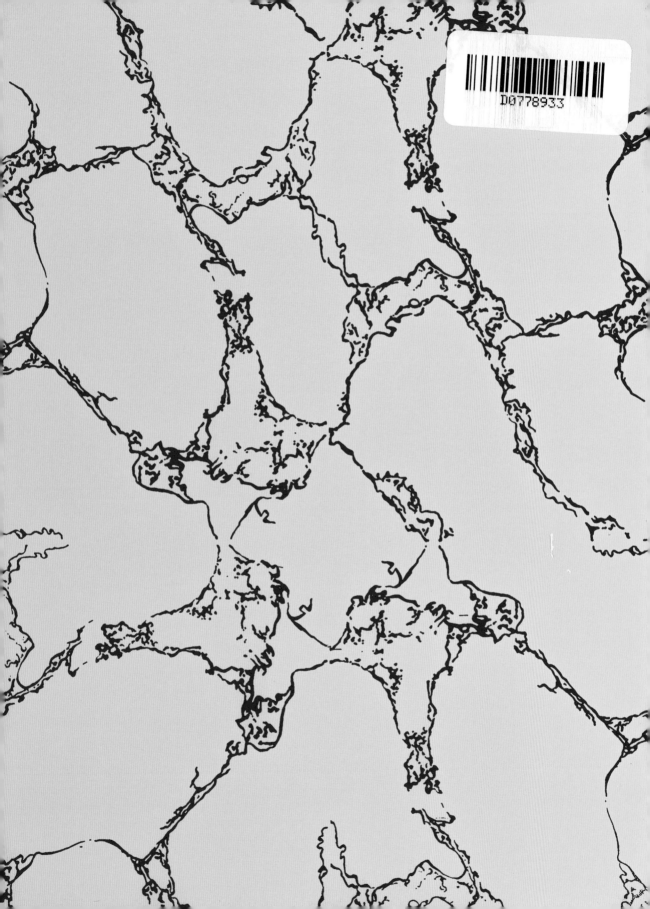

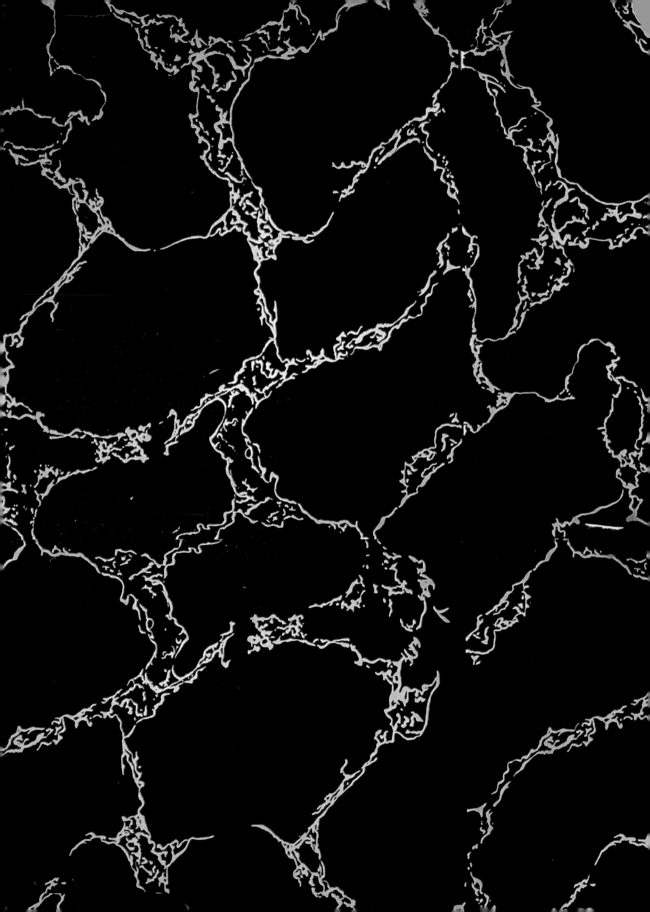

Melt, Stretch, & Sizzle

THE ART OF COOKING

Cheese

Tia Keenan

Foreword by Kat Kinsman

RIZZOLI
NEW YORK

New York · Paris · London · Milan

First published in the United States of America in 2018
by Rizzoli International Publications, Inc.
300 Park Avenue South
New York, NY 10010
www.rizzoliusa.com

© 2018 by Tia Keenan
tiakeenan.com

Photographs © Noah Fecks
noahfecks.com

Food styling by Victoria Granof
victoriagranof.com

Prop styling by Christopher Spaulding, Reclaim Design
rcdnyc.com

Design by Lynne Yeamans

2018 2019 2020 2021 / 10 9 8 7 6 5 4 3 2 1

Distributed to the U.S. trade by Random House, New York
Printed in China

ISBN-13: 978-0-7893-3442-8
Library of Congress Catalog Control Number: 2018937800

Contents

Foreword by Kat Kinsman 8

Introduction: Melt with Me 10

SAUCY 16

SIZZLERS 30

DIP IN 42

LIVE & LET FRY 60

SANDWHATEVERS 82

'SUP, SOUP? 102

POTATO HEAD 118

PASTA LOVERS 136

CHEESE, AIR, SEX, MAGIC 152

RACLETTE'S GET IT ON 168

Index 187

Sources 191

Acknowledgments 192

Recipes & Sidebars

Mornay Sauce 18

Swiss Fondue 21

Rarebit Sauce 22

   Rarebitten 24

   *What You Gonna Do
with All That Dunk?* 25

Truffle Fonduta 27

Blue Cheese Sauce 28

Halloumi Flambé with
Preserved Lemon & Basil 32

Bread Cheese with Tamari, Maple,
& Thai Chiles 35

Queso de Freir with Guava Paste
& Oregano Oil 37

Paneer in Minted Pea Sauce 38

   Grilling Cheeses 40

   *Get with the Pan: Why I Love
Cast-Iron* 41

Baked Ricotta with Fresh Herbs 45

Baked Feta with Pickled Peppers
& Dill 46

   *A Quick Recipe for Pita or
Flatbread Chips* 49

   Global Feta-ration 48

Baked Pumpkin Fondue 50

Cheese Blends for Great Pumpkins 53

Baked Brie Kataifi with Honey 55

   Get Bloomy & Baked 56

   Spoon Cheeses: Dip Right In 57

Goat Cheese Queso Fundido 58

Fried Burrata with Roasted
Tomatoes 62

Fried Chèvre 67

   Quick Parsley Sauce 68

   A Year of Fried Chèvre Salads 69

Fried Cheese Curds 70

   *Buffalo Curds with Blue Cheese
Dip* 72

Little Dutch Eggs 75

Malakoff 78

   A Quick Guide to Frying Oils 80

   Cheddar, Interrupted 81

American-Style Grilled Cheese 85

   Grilled Cheese How-to 86

BuffArepa 89

   *For a Truly Great Grilled Cheese,
Mix It Up!* 91

Pljeskavica 93

Francesinha 94

Thanksgiving Francesinha 96

Grilled Cheese Inspirations for When You're Feeling Extra 97

Khachipuri 98

Red Wines for Khachipuri 101

French Onion Soup 105

Stock Tips: A Simple Guide to Making Stock 107

Colcannon Stew with Bacon & Blue Cheese 108

Flavor & Fat: The "Lowdown" on Cooking with Blue Cheese 110

Broccoli Cheddar Soup 111

Potato, Cheese, & Corn Soup 114

Cream, Get on Top: Fresh Cheeses for Filling & Finishing 117

Aligot 120

Potato Gratin with Pancetta & Leeks 123

Finishing Cheeses: Like Salt, like Breadcrumbs, but Cheese 125

Chorizo, Egg, & Cheese Baked Potato 126

Welcome to the Melt, Stretch, & Sizzle Baked Potato Bar, How May I Help You? 129

Poutine with Lazy Gravy 131

Frico 132

Another Day, Another Frico 135

Burrata Mac & Cheese 139

Cheese Manicotti 4G 140

Käsespätzle 144

The Official Bev of Bavaria: Beer 147

Kugel with Cottage Cheese, Leeks, & Dill 148

Mac & Cheese Combinations to Win Friends & Influence People 151

Classic Cheese Soufflé 155

Seriously: Don't. Open. The Oven. 156

Gougères 157

White Wines (+ Beers) for Gougères 160

Popover Country 161

Smoked Gouda & Bacon Dutch Baby 162

Pecorino Popover 164

Pão de Queijo 167

There's More Than One Way to Raclette 173

Raclette It All 174

American Raclette 175

French Connection 176

American Ingenuity 179

Melt the Moon 180

Italian Feast 183

FOREWORD

At the core of my food philosophy is one simple tenet: If it tastes good, it is good. How that actually plays out is that I've got endless respect for people's likes and dislikes, especially when it comes to what they eat. But if they don't dig cheese, I can't pretend I'm not morbidly curious about why exactly. If they're vegan or lactose intolerant, sure, I get that. But otherwise, seriously—*what's not to love*?

Tia Keenan is having none of this. She's a woman on a fromage mission, fueled by a deep, genuine desire to see people lose their freaking minds over cheese.

There are few people more qualified to lead this quest than Tia Keenan. She's spent her entire career kicking at the fussy margins of conventional cheese wisdom for the express purpose of helping people enjoy it even more. Running the cheese program at the Michelin-starred restaurant The Modern at The Museum of Modern Art, she steered the cheese cart in an infinitely funkier, more playful direction, outside the fine-dining, Euro-centric boundaries the diners were used to, and they came along gleefully. At Casellula Cheese & Wine Café in Hell's Kitchen, she furthered her following by exploring mind-bending pairings that honored and elevated the craft of the cheesemakers she tirelessly champions. And by the time she opened New York's first cheese bar with the venerable Murray's Cheese in the West Village, the city's dairy devotees were pounding at the door to get in.

There's something about Tia that makes people go all gooey in her presence. It's not just her ever-evolving expertise, her twinkly-eyed risk taking, nor her tireless advocacy for the artisans who craft the product she's devoted her life to. It's that she truly wants everyone else to be getting as big a thrill out of life as she is, and cheese is how she gets her kicks.

Give a person a fish and they eat for a day. Teach them how to build a cheese plate, and they'll throw legendary soirees for the rest of their life. In her first book, *The Art of the Cheese Plate: Pairings, Recipes, Style, Attitude,* Tia empowered even novice cheese lovers to better understand their own passions and proclivities to craft the experience that would bring them and their guests the most delight. It's artful, innovative, and an absolute must for the library of any cheese lover.

And *Melt, Stretch & Sizzle: The Art of Cooking Cheese* is the hot, sweaty, shoes-kicked-off and grinding on the dance floor after-party. As Tia notes straight off the bat, hot cheese just does something to people. This is a lust letter to the physicality of the stuff—the pure abandon of giving yourself over to the melty, gooey, drippy, messy pleasure of it all.

Contemplate the raclette for a second. The communal ritual of melting cheese over a bounty of foods is at the top of Tia's last-meal checklist, but it may be unfamiliar to many who grew up outside the tradition. It's just so very Tia, though—gathering people together around a table laden with all the things they want to eat, and giving people everything they need to make themselves and one another happy. And she's not satisfied to just leave it at that. Once she's taught you the basics and specifics, she gives you the tools to level up and make it yours. And fondue? Oh yes, she does—and savory rarebit, and truffled-up fonduta, and luscious potato-amped aligot, poutine aplenty, and every global variation of grilled cheese.

And can we talk for a sec about how gorgeous this book looks? If you're anything like me and grew up poring over the Time Life series of culinary and entertaining books, dreaming of how glamorous your life was going to be someday, this is your happy place. It's cheekily elegant and entirely achievable for amateurs who are seeking to add a little cheese porn to their collection. This is the grownup life I always wanted to achieve, and Tia is grabbing me by the hand and leading me there. (I go willingly.)

But it's not just the ooze and pull and *mmmmmmmm*—Tia is a master of her subject and she's a natural and generous teacher. She wants you to be as head-over-heels in love with cheese as she is, so she gives you her full arsenal, which includes technique, recipes, and even brands—which is also so Tia, because she wants the people who actually make the worthwhile stuff to join the party, too.

This is Tia's world and it's cheesy as hell—or possibly heaven—and I'm here to tell you, it is good.

Go get messy.

—KAT KINSMAN

Melt with Me

I wrote this book to explore the transformative energy of heat applied to cheese, both what happens to the cheese and what happens to us: the lust, adoration, excitement, and pleasure that melt inspires. This is my ode to cheese porn.

With straightforward, crave-worthy recipes as my starting point, my goal is to share basic concepts and techniques with you while teasing out a deeper appreciation of why all things melty, oozy, and gooey captivate us. I haven't created anything close to a definitive compendium. Instead, I've gathered a personal and somewhat eclectic collection of recipes I consider foundational, fun, foolproof, and worthy of the hot cheese canon. It's my homage to a food and experience I've loved since I was a tot, when my mother recorded in my baby book that grilled cheese was my favorite food.

I've spent many hours of my work life, as a chef and fromager, listening to ordinary people—strangers, usually—confess their lust for raclette, how far they'd go for fondue, or the indulgences they'd forgo for another bite of baked Brie. More than once I've heard someone say, "Grilled cheese is better than sex." Seriously? Seriously. I've seen a young, beautiful man ignore his equally young, beautiful date once a plate of hot cheese curds hit the table. I've witnessed a woman of a certain age groan with unbridled pleasure while guiding a forkful of cheesy pasta toward her eager mouth. Hot cheese just does something to people.

THE SCIENCE OF HOT CHEESE

You probably don't need a recipe to make a simple grilled cheese. But you do need a cheese that melts well, and not all of them do. In order to cook successfully with cheese—to get the kind of melt (or nonmelt) you want for a recipe—it's helpful to have an understanding of the basic science of hot cheese.

In the beginning of the cheese-making process, milk is heated along with a coagulant—either acid (usually vinegar or citric acid from lemon juice) or rennet (an enzyme harvested from the stomach lining of young ruminants). The heat and coagulant combination causes the main protein in milk, called casein, to capture fat and water molecules in a three-dimensional web—a ménage à trois of protein, fat, and water. The strength or weakness of the bonds in this threesome and the ratio of the fat and water content are the primary indicators of how a cheese will melt. In general, high-moisture cheeses with weaker protein structure melt well; low-moisture cheeses with stronger, more compact protein structures do not.

At a party featuring hot cheese, acid-set cheeses are the members of the ménage that go awry (see **Sizzlers**, page 30). The proteins are so tightly bonded that fat and water don't "get off"—they refuse to melt. The acid kills the mood for melting. Whether the cheese is acid-set by style (such as ricotta) or naturally acidic (such as chèvre), the proteins are too tightly wound to get all the way down.

Rennet-set cheeses, however, especially high-moisture, young, and middle-aged cheeses, have casein bonds that don't tense up when heat energy is applied—they break down and loosen up. Loose protein, fat, and water bonds? This is the threesome that gets cheeseheads gooey.

Milk fat begins to melt around 90°F, and as the temperature climbs, the structures of the casein—the bonds that hold it together—begin to break down, releasing the fat and water and "liquefying" the cheese. High-moisture cheeses, like mozzarella, melt at about 130°F; aged cheeses, like Gruyère and cheddar, at about 150°F; and low-moisture and aged cheeses, like Parmesan, at around 180°F.

COOKING VS. CHEESE-PLATE CHEESES

A trend that began several years ago is cooking with more exclusive (read: expensive) cheeses. Stop the insanity! A $30-per-pound cheese made on a small farm from a rare breed of cows should not go bulk into baked pasta (as a Finishing Cheese, see page 125, maybe, but not more than that). A special, rare, pricey cheese is a finished product, to be savored on a cheese plate or maybe served as a fondue (see page 21) or raclette (see **Raclette's Get It On**, page 168). If a recipe calls for more than four ounces of a particular cheese, stick with something reasonably priced that's intended for cooking.

Generally, a combination of affordable supermarket cheeses with an occasional and strategic smattering of slightly pricier specialty cheeses will get you the flavor and melt that you want. Most hot cheese recipes—both in this book and more generally—are best when made with:

- ACTUAL CHEESE: made from milk, salt, and rennet;

- CHEESE THAT HAS SOME KIND OF FLAVOR DEVELOPMENT (I.E. CHEESE THAT DOESN'T TASTE LIKE PLASTIC); AND

- CHEESE THAT IS EASY TO FIND AND AFFORDABLE.

Understanding the basics of cooking cheeses will also help guide you when you want to swap cheeses in a specific recipe for cheeses you already have hanging out in your fridge.

CONSIDER THE FOLLOWING WHEN CHOOSING CHEESES TO COOK WITH:

The MELT a dish requires.

- DO YOU WANT A STRINGY, GOOEY, OOZY MELTER FOR BURRATA MAC & CHEESE (PAGE 139)?

- OR SOMETHING STABLE THAT WILL HOLD TOGETHER FOR CHEESE MANICOTTI 4G (PAGE 140)?

What FLAVOR a dish requires.

- DO YOU WANT A TANGY, BRIGHT, SALTY CHEESE FOR KHACHIPURI (PAGE 98)?

- OR A MILD, EARTHY CHEESE FOR TRUFFLE FONDUTA (PAGE 27)?

The QUANTITY of cheese you'll need and its APPLICATION in the dish.

- JUST A TABLESPOON OR TWO TO FINISH A DISH? SPLURGE ON PARMIGIANO REGGIANO (SEE POTATO GRATIN WITH PANCETTA & LEEKS, PAGE 123).

- RECIPE CALLS FOR A LARGER AND POTENTIALLY COSTLIER QUANTITY OF CHEESE?

Once you've determined what kind of cheese you need, it's time to head to the market. With cooking cheeses that will often mean the supermarket. Of course many supermarkets sell an abundance of specialty cheeses now, but when I mention supermarket cheeses, I'm referring to cheeses typically found in the dairy or deli aisles.

SUPERMARKET CHEESES: THE HOLY GRAIL OF HOT CHEESE

Here's a rundown of the basic categories of cheese found at the supermarket. You can make most of the recipes in this book with these cheeses.

- **FILLING CHEESES** (*cheeses that make a base or filling*)**:**
  ricotta, cottage cheese, feta, chèvre, queso fresco, cream cheese
  (see Cream, Get on Top, page 117)
- **YOUNG CHEESES:** mozzarella and soft-ripened cheese like Brie
- **SEMI-FIRM CHEESES:** fontina, Gouda, Havarti
- **FIRM CHEESES:** cheddar, Jarlsberg, Swiss
- **BLUE CHEESES:** Danish blue, Gorgonzola, and other high-moisture blue cheeses
  (see The Lowdown on Cooking with Blue Cheese, page 110)

HOW TO USE THE CHEESE NOTES WITH THE RECIPES

Underneath the title of each recipe, you'll see one or more of the following notes, meant to help you choose the cheeses for the specific recipe.

- **TRADITIONAL:** Recommends a specific cheese closely tied to a specific recipe.
- **SUBSTITUTION:** Recommends cheeses that are suitable to replace the traditional cheese noted.

- **RECOMMENDED:** For recipes that are less traditional, an array of cheeses that are suitable.
- **TRUSTED BRAND:** Brands deserving a specific callout for reliability, consistency, and availability.

When the name of the cheese is in the title of the recipe and/or there's no substitution or recommended brand, there is no note about the cheese: use what the recipe indicates in the ingredient list. When there's flexibility in the cheese selection—denoted by the notes underneath the recipe title—the cheese is referred to in the recipe as "cheese of choice." In other words, you pick the cheese based on the cheese notes at the top of the recipe.

INSTRUMENTS OF MELT: COOKING EQUIPMENT

Controlling temperature—cooking at the temperature you want and maintaining that temperature throughout the process—is an essential cooking skill, and it's crucial when cooking with cheese. For the money, no other type of pan heats as evenly, or maintains temperature as consistently, as a cast-iron pan. In almost all of the recipes, I recommend either a cast-iron or a "heavy-bottomed" pan, which could be enamel-coated cast-iron, a copper-bottomed pan, or any other pan that heats evenly and holds heat well.

A well-seasoned, oft-used cast-iron pan is also nonstick, which is especially helpful since cooked cheese can act like glue when heated and cooled. Nothing is better for cooking a grilled cheese than a cast-iron pan: for heat control, toasting, flavor (cast-iron imparts a bit of saltiness onto the bread whilst cooking), and cleanup.

THE LAST STEP: ADJUST YOUR SEASONING

It can't be stressed enough that cheese is a salted, prepared ingredient. In almost all cheese-centric and cheese-heavy recipes, the amount of salt needed will vary depending on the exact cheese you use—down to the specific brand and batch, to be really geeky about it. For these recipes, I settled somewhere in the middle of the salt scale, recommending an amount of salt that I knew would not oversalt the specific recipe (no matter what cheese you use) with plenty of reminders throughout the recipes to taste and adjust seasoning. In a few recipes, salt isn't included because the cheese is salty enough.

A FINAL NOTE ON HOT CHEESE ADORATION AND FANTASY

I don't know why I chose cheese as my medium of self-expression so many years ago, but I know it had something to do with loving something that so many other people love too, and the pleasure this shared adoration brings me. When I work with cheese I'm inviting others to step into my world.

Melt, Stretch, & Sizzle is my love letter to hot cheese, inspired by the enthusiasm cheese lovers have shared with me over the years. It's an homage to every groan of pleasure inspired by a mac and cheese, to every squeal brought on by a plate of hot, crispy fried cheese curds. This is my way of giving back to all my fellow cheese lovers. I don't just want to melt cheese, I want you to melt with me. Let's ride on a wave of molten cheese, to a fantastical land where the cheddar is hot, the mozzarella is bubbling, and we're free to eat what we love with unabashed pleasure.

CHEESE SAUCES ARE THE GATEWAY TO UNDERSTANDING SOME of the basic rules of melt. Once you know how to whip up a hot cheese sauce, the question becomes not what you'll pour them on, but what you won't. Because you're only limited by your own sense of decency. Almost everything tastes better draped in the luscious lava of liquefied cheese.

Cheese sauces fall into three main categories: roux-thickened sauces (Mornay and rarebit), starch-thickened sauces (fondue), and cream-and-egg-thickened sauces (fonduta and blue cheese). A tablespoon of cream cheese is a restaurant trick that stabilizes cheese sauces of any ilk without altering the flavor or texture. (Don't tell a French person I recommend this, as it may get me banned from that fantasyland of fromage—*quelle horreur*!). Add the cream cheese in during the last few minutes of cooking.

Time plays an important role in successful cheese sauces. Not time in the sense of long duration, but in the sense of being deliberate, not working sloppily or rushing. A cheese sauce on a tight deadline is a recipe for disaster—you'll inevitably want to cheat the temperature maintenance, ending up with something stringy and soupy instead of silken and sexy. Here's a jingle to help you:

Make the time
Cheese sauce sublime

Drastic temperature fluctuation is the enemy of able-bodied cheese sauces. Your goal should be "smooth transition." Temper your cheese by leaving it at room temperature for a half hour and add it to the recipe incrementally. A mess of cold cheese dropped into hot liquid pretty much guarantees a broken sauce. It's vital to keep your sauce in a temperature range that's friendly to emulsification. And proper emulsification is the difference between a smooth, creamy sauce and a tragic, broken glop.

Lastly, once you've finished making your cheese sauce, serve it immediately or keep it warm using gentle, well-regulated heat. Fondue pots, double boilers, and heavy-bottomed pans are invaluable for maintaining a steady "hold" temperature.

Mornay Sauce

BASIC BITCH

TRADITIONAL: *Gruyère or Comté*

SUBSTITUTIONS: *alpine or alpine-style cheeses such as Spring Brook Farm Tarentaise or Uplands Cheese Pleasant Ridge Reserve*

A Mornay is a classic roux-thickened cheese sauce made from a béchamel, one of the five "mother sauces" in classic French cuisine. It's ready to engulf any number of vegetables, and it's also used in Burrata Mac & Cheese (page 139) and Chorizo, Egg, & Cheese Baked Potato (page 126).

4 tablespoons (½ stick) unsalted butter

¼ cup plus 1 tablespoon all-purpose flour

¼ teaspoon kosher salt

¼ teaspoon freshly ground white pepper

⅛ teaspoon freshly grated nutmeg

3 cups whole milk

1 bay leaf

4 ounces cheese of choice, shredded (about 1 cup), at room temperature

In a medium heavy-bottomed saucepan over medium heat, melt the butter. Add the flour and whisk continuously until the roux is the color of roasted cashews and has a nutty aroma, about 3 minutes. Whisk in the salt, white pepper, and nutmeg, then pour in the milk, whisking continuously. Add the bay leaf.

Reduce the heat to medium-low and simmer until thickened, whisking occasionally, about 8 minutes (the sauce should coat the back of a wooden spoon and have the consistency of drinkable yogurt). Discard the bay leaf.

Gradually whisk the cheese into the sauce in two big handfuls, adding more cheese only after the previous handful is incorporated. Once all the cheese is melted, cook for 1 more minute to assure all of the cheese is emulsified into the sauce (this would also be the time to add a tablespoon of cream cheese as insurance against breakage if you're feeling you need it). Season with salt and white pepper if needed and serve immediately.

Makes 3 cups cheesy manna for your pouring pleasure

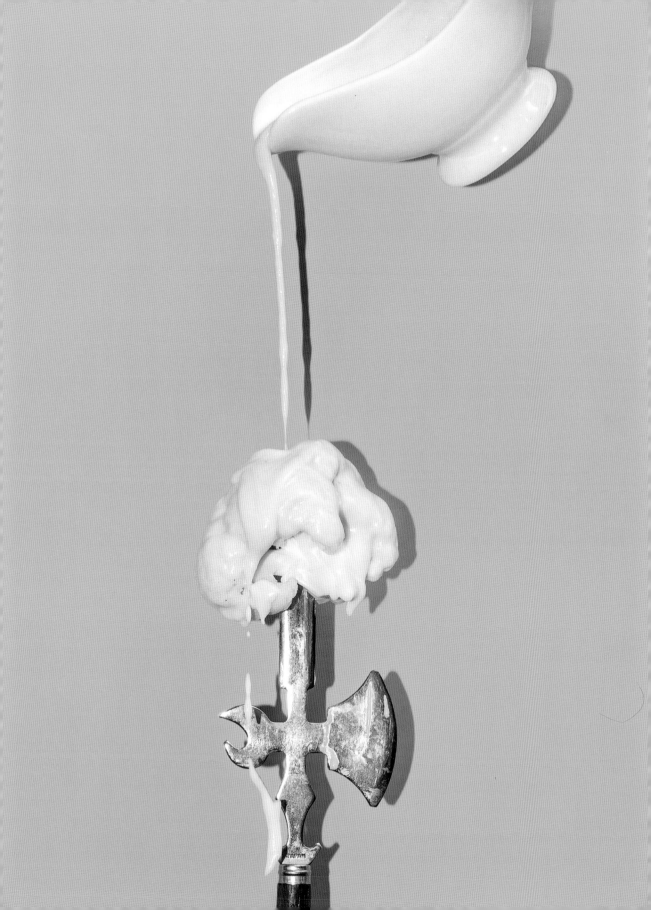

Swiss Fondue

CLASSIC GIRL

TRADITIONAL: *Gruyère*

SUBSTITUTIONS: *alpine or alpine-style cheeses such as Comté, Spring Brook Farm Tarentaise, or Uplands Cheese Pleasant Ridge Reserve*

The first modern recipe for fondue appeared in a seventeenth-century Swiss cookbook *To Cook with Cheese and Wine*, an apt debut since fondue is a wine-based cheese sauce. Like many classic hot cheese dishes, it's the work of peasants looking to stretch a meal, in this case with odd bits of cheese, over-the-hill wine, and stale bread.

1½ pounds cheese of choice, shredded (about 6 cups), at room temperature

2 tablespoons cornstarch

½ teaspoon freshly grated nutmeg

1 garlic clove

2 cups dry white wine

2 tablespoons kirsch (optional)

In a large bowl, toss the cheese with the cornstarch and nutmeg. Rub a medium heavy-bottomed saucepan (enamel-coated works especially well here) or fondue pot with the garlic clove, then discard it.

Add the wine to the saucepan and bring it to a simmer over medium heat. Gradually whisk the cheese into the wine a handful at a time, adding more cheese only after the previous handful is incorporated. Once all the cheese is incorporated, cook for 1 more minute, then stir in the kirsch, if you like, for an additional layer of boozy flavor. Serve immediately, with lots of delicious things to dip into it.

Makes 3 cups alpine silk

Rarebit Sauce

PEASANT PLEASURE

TRADITIONAL: *English cheddar or Cotswold*
SUBSTITUTIONS: *5 Spoke Creamery Tumbleweed, Beehive Cheese Co. Apple Walnut Smoked Cheddar*

Consider rarebit sauce the ruddy English cousin of Swiss boarding school fondue. It's a beer-laced, roux- and egg yolk–thickened sauce that plays the role of "meat" in Welsh rarebit, a simple dish of toasted bread and rarebit sauce. It's more deeply flavored than a Mornay, with a malty, spiced kick that's excellent on roasted root vegetables and hearty rye toast alike. Sometimes rough-and-tumble is just right.

2 tablespoons unsalted butter	½ cup dark beer, such as a stout
2 tablespoons all-purpose flour	1 tablespoon Worcestershire sauce
½ teaspoon kosher salt	¾ cup heavy cream
¼ teaspoon ground mustard	1 egg yolk
⅛ teaspoon freshly ground black pepper	6 ounces cheese of choice, shredded (about 1½ cups), at room temperature
⅛ teaspoon cayenne pepper	

In a medium, heavy-bottomed saucepan over medium heat, melt the butter until foaming. Add the flour and whisk continuously until the roux is the color of roasted cashews and has a nutty aroma, about 2 minutes. Whisk in the salt, mustard, black pepper, and cayenne, then the beer and Worcestershire.

Cook, stirring, until the sauce thickens, another 2 to 3 minutes, then add the heavy cream and cook another 2 minutes to bring the mixture to a simmer. In a small bowl, mix a few tablespoons of the hot cream mixture into the egg yolk (this tempers the egg yolk so it emulsifies into the sauce instead of scrambling), then whisk it all back into the sauce.

Whisk the cheese into the sauce in three batches, adding more cheese only after the previous batch is incorporated. Once all the cheese is melted, cook, stirring once or twice, for another 5 minutes to thicken. Adjust seasoning if needed and serve immediately.

Makes 1½ cups beer-tastic lava

Rarebitten.

The popular lore surrounding Welsh rarebit hinges on the etymology of "rarebit," namely that it's a corruption of "rabbit." The story goes that Welsh peasants were forbidden from eating rabbits trapped on land owned by gentry, and so named their humble snack of cheesy toast "rarebit" (as in "cheese is the poor man's rabbit"). There's not much evidence to support this story other than its persistence through the ages, but its subversive humor is spot-on, and who doesn't love a cheese pun?

WELSH RAREBIT

Thick-cut toast under rarebit sauce, broiled until browned. Best paired with a pint of your favorite dark brew, of course.

BUCK RABBIT

Thick-cut toast under rarebit sauce, broiled until browned, with a poached or sunny-side up egg. "British Brunch" (or Her Majesty's Hangover Cure) is served.

RAREBIT BURGER

Thick-cut toast topped with a griddled hamburger, under rarebit sauce. A cheeseburger is born! Thick-cut fries on the side, please, to soak up extra sauce.

RAREBIT BAKED POTATO

A perfectly baked potato under rarebit sauce, with crumbled bacon, clotted cream, and a flurry of chives, makes a gluten-free rarebit to get down with.

What You Gonna Do with All That Dunk?

Cheese sauces can be daintily poured or brutishly slathered on all types of foods, but they can also serve as fondue by proxy. It's as simple as rigging a hot pot of cheese sauce, curating a killer selection of tasty foods to bathe, slather, dip, and dunk, and congratulating yourself on the brilliance that is low-effort, big-impact (and even frugal) eating and entertaining. A few of my favorite combinations:

THE CLASSICS

Stick with the classics when serving fondue, opting for boiled baby potatoes, cubes of toasted baguette, cornichons, and some ham or dried sausage.

RAREBIT

For rarebit, skew toward more robust flavors to clap back at the malty depth of the sauce. Grilled sausages, roasted sweet potatoes, pickled pearl onions, and cubes of dark rye or pumpernickel bread are good, hearty choices.

FONDUTA

Fonduta is a delicately flavored sauce that's all about the richness of cream, eggs, butter, and cheese. Tread lightly by dunking roasted mushrooms, focaccia flecked with rosemary, or cubes of griddled polenta.

BLUE CHEESE SAUCE

Go for the gusto with Blue Cheese Sauce! My favorite to dip is grilled, roasted, or cured meats. Roasted chicken, grilled steak tips, and bresaola (Italian air-dried beef) all fit the bill. If meat isn't your thing and you're not afraid to experiment, prunes and apricots plumped up with a bit of brandy are surprisingly delightful.

Truffle Fonduta

LUX TERROIR

TRADITIONAL: *Fontina Valle d'Aosta*
SUBSTITUTION: *fontina*

Although Switzerland and France are the countries most commonly associated with the Alps, Italy also borders this mountain region known for its superlative cheeses. Fonduta is Italy's holler-back to Swiss fondue, by way of Piedmont and Valle d'Aosta. More custardy than the Swiss version (shout-out to eggs, cream, and butter!), it's typically spooned over roasted vegetables or polenta. The addition of truffles makes this particular iteration of fonduta a fire worth feeding.

3 egg yolks

2 tablespoons unsalted butter

1 cup heavy cream

8 ounces cheese of choice, shredded (about 2 cups), at room temperature

1 small, fresh truffle (go with what the season and your wallet will allow)

Salt and freshly ground black pepper

Whisk the egg yolks in a small bowl and set aside.

Melt the butter in a medium saucepan over medium heat. Add the cream and cook until simmering, about 3 minutes. Whisk the cheese into the hot cream in three batches, adding more cheese only after the previous batch is incorporated.

Once the cheese melts into the cream, mix a few tablespoons of the hot cream mixture into the egg yolks, then whisk it all back into the sauce. (If you're using black or summer truffles, shave them in now with a Microplane zester.) Cook until the sauce thickens, 3 to 4 minutes. Remove from the heat.

If you're using white truffles, shave them into the sauce with a truffle shaver or Microplane zester off the heat, to preserve their more delicate flavor. Season with salt and pepper if needed and serve immediately.

Makes 1½ cups creamy goodness, get on top

Blue Cheese Sauce

UMAMI BATH

TRADITIONAL: *Gorgonzola, Stilton, or Roquefort*
SUBSTITUTIONS: *Jasper Hill Farm Bayley Hazen Blue or Old Chatham Sheepherding Ewe's Blue*

The best cheese for this sauce depends entirely on what you intend to bathe in it. For lighter foods, such as pasta or chicken, Gorgonzola (both Cremificato or dolce) is a mild, delicately flavored choice. Heartier fare, such as roast beef or potatoes, can benefit from a more intensely flavored sauce made from bolder blues, such as Roquefort and Stilton. Remember to consider the saltiness of your cheese of choice and adjust the seasoning of the foods you'll be blanketing accordingly.

1 tablespooon unsalted butter

1 small shallot, finely diced (¼ cup)

1 garlic clove

1 cup heavy cream

1 egg yolk

5 ounces blue cheese, crumbled (about ¾ cup), at room temperature

Salt and freshly ground black pepper

In a small saucepan over medium-low heat, melt the butter until foaming. Add the shallot and garlic and cook until the shallot is translucent, about 3 minutes.

Add the cream, increase the heat to medium-high, and bring to a boil, then reduce the heat to low and simmer, stirring occasionally, until the mixture is reduced by half and has turned slightly yellow, about 12 minutes.

In a separate small bowl, mix a few tablespoons of the hot cream mixture into the egg yolk, then whisk it all back into the sauce. Whisk the cheese into the sauce in two batches, whisking continuously and adding more cheese only after the previous batch is incorporated. For a completely smooth sauce, you may have to break up some of the larger blue cheese crumbles with a spoon, though a slightly chunky sauce can also be nice. Season with salt and pepper if needed and serve immediately.

Makes 1 cup molten umami

SIZZLERS KEEP IT TIGHT WHEN THE HEAT IS ON, REFUSING TO melt no matter how hot things get. Seared in a pan, grilled, or doused in booze and set alight (because nothing says "Party!" like flaming cheese), these mild, firm, acid-set cheeses absorb whatever flavors are tossed at them—and get crisp and charred to boot. Their seemingly endless adaptability makes up for their obstinate lack of ooze. These babies are ready for the frying pan and the fire.

Admittedly, cheeses that are more sizzle than melt may not immediately come to mind when fantasizing about hot cheese, but these outliers deserve a closer look. (It's okay to admit you've fantasized about hot cheese before. Anyone who says they haven't is lying.)

Sizzlers run with a fast crowd—going from refrigerator-cool to party-hot in fifteen minutes. They're typically sold in vacuum-sealed packaging and will happily chill for several months in the fridge until you need them, then cook up faster than you can say "hot cheese." They're a great back-pocket party trick for impromptu entertaining.

Punctuating flavors—whether from spice or acidity—are a must. These mild cheeses demand bold flourishes, so don't be afraid to use some. Sizzlers also go both ways: sweet and savory applications work equally well. Spicy is nice, as are bright takes with a hit of acidity and lots of fresh herbs. Just keep it relatively simple. Dress them in too many accessories and their mild manner gets lost in the hullabaloo.

Halloumi Flambé with Preserved Lemon & Basil

BURNING LOVE

TRUSTED BRAND: *Mt Vikos*

Halloumi is a compact, cream-colored brick of cheese from Cyprus that derives its saltiness from brine. Originally made exclusively of a blend of goat and sheep's milk, or solely of goat or sheep's milk, modern halloumi is often an amalgam of goat, sheep, or cow's milk or even solely cow's milk. Confusing, right? Avoid the confusion by buying whatever's available—all permutations work well here.

If you've never flambéed before, don't fret; just make sure you're in a well-ventilated area a good distance away from any heat source. Pour the booze on the cheese, then carefully hit it with a stick lighter or long match, stand back, and let it burn, baby. It shouldn't smoke much, and the flame will burn down with the alcohol, but have a lid handy, too—covering the pan will quickly extinguish the flame.

1 (8-ounce) piece halloumi

1 tablespoon olive oil

1 teaspoon diced preserved lemon

2 tablespoons limoncello

8 basil leaves, finely chopped (about ¼ cup)

Fresh lemon wedges, for serving

Place a medium cast-iron or sauté pan over medium heat until very hot, about 5 minutes. Rub the halloumi with the olive oil, add it to the hot skillet, and immediately turn the heat up to medium-high. Sear the cheese until deeply browned on one side, about 4 minutes.

Flip and continue to cook for 2 more minutes, then add the preserved lemon to the pan, pour the limoncello over the cheese, and set aflame with a stick lighter or long match. Stand back and cook undisturbed for 1 or 2 minutes more, until the alcohol burns off.

Transfer to a serving platter, garnish with the basil and lemon wedges, and serve immediately.

Serves 2 flame lovers

Bread Cheese with Tamari, Maple, & Thai Chiles

(IT'S BREADLESS)

Wisconsin is the bread cheese basket of America, but its origins are in Finland and Sweden (where it's called juustoleipä or leipäjuusto). Prebaked during production, the resulting browning on top of the finished cheese looks uncannily like a baked loaf of bread. Bread cheese only needs to be warmed through before serving, so move quickly: you want to heat the cheese without losing its structural integrity. Too much heat will overly soften it, making the cheese more blobby than springy. Sweet and spicy Asian-tinged flavors are a welcome surprise for a Scandinavian-born, Wisconsin-bred cheese.

1 teaspoon fresh lime juice

1 teaspoon tamari or soy sauce

1 teaspoon maple syrup (the darker the better)

1 teaspoon sesame oil

2 garlic cloves, thinly sliced

2 Thai bird's eye chiles, sliced (for less heat, substitute serrano peppers)

10 ounces bread cheese, cut into ¾-inch cubes

1 teaspoon crushed red pepper flakes

2 scallions, chopped

2 tablespoons toasted sesame seeds

In a small bowl, whisk the lime juice, tamari, and maple syrup and set aside.

Preheat a medium cast-iron or sauté pan over medium heat. Add the sesame oil to the hot pan, then add the garlic and chiles and cook until fragrant, about 1 minute. Turn the heat to medium-high, add the lime juice mixture, and cook for another 1 to 2 minutes, until the sauce has reduced by one-third. Add the cheese cubes, toss in the red pepper flakes, and cook until the cheese is hot and the sauce thickens, 2 to 3 more minutes.

Garnish with the scallions and sesame seeds and serve immediately. It's fun to serve these in a multitude of little cups with toothpicks for easy spearing, but it can also be served on a platter.

Serves 4 snackers or 2 gluttons

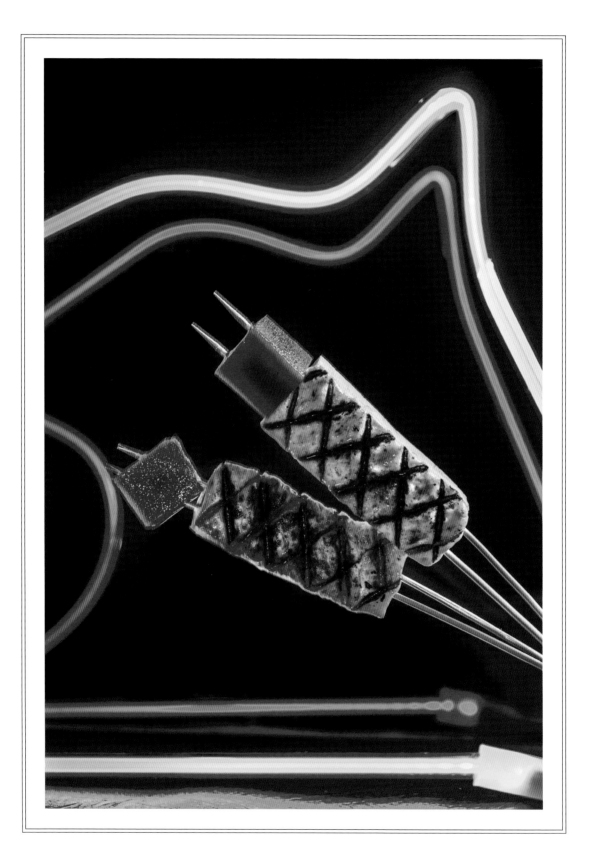

Queso de Freir with Guava Paste & Oregano Oil

FAST, CHEAP, & EASY

TRUSTED BRAND: *Tropical*

Queso de freir is a variation of queso blanco: a simple, acid-set cheese made from cow's milk that is common throughout the United States, Mexico, and Central and South America. It's a classic "bodega cheese," which means you can score the main ingredients for this sweet and savory snack from your corner shop at two o'clock in the morning and be on your couch consuming it twenty minutes later. You don't have to be rich to rule my world.

4 wooden skewers

1 (12-ounce) package queso de freir, cut lengthwise into ½-inch-thick slices

½ cup olive oil

4 sprigs fresh oregano

1 garlic clove, unpeeled

4 ounces Goya guava paste, cut into 4 1-inch cubes

Freshly ground black pepper

Soak skewers in water for 15 minutes. Thread the cheese onto skewers.

In a small saucepan over low heat, warm the olive oil, oregano, and garlic for 10 minutes. Remove the pan from the heat, strain the oil into a small bowl, and discard the solids.

Heat a medium cast-iron grill pan or skillet, or sauté pan, over medium heat. Add 2 tablespoons of the oregano oil and heat until fragrant and shimmering. Sear the cheese skewers on all sides, cooking for 6 to 7 minutes total. Drain on a plate lined with paper towels.

Silde a cube of guava paste onto the skewers, drizzle with some of the remaining oil, season with black pepper, and serve immediately.

Serves 4 for bodega eleganza

Paneer in Minted Pea Sauce

PASSAGE TO INDIA

TRUSTED BRAND: *Amul*

Paneer is a mild, acid-set cow's milk cheese indigenous to the northwestern part of South Asia. The most familiar paneer to the American palate is found in Indian restaurants across the United States in the form of saag paneer, chunks of the mild panfried cheese in an aromatic sauce of leafy greens. This make-at-home take has a cooler, lighter vibe more suitable for an appetizer, with a creamy buttermilk pea sauce brightened by lemon and mint. It's a simple yet sophisticated take on an Indian staple, and a chance to get to know a cheese that's affordable, versatile, and, because of its very mild flavor, a veritable blank canvas.

2 tablespoons coconut oil

1 (8-ounce) package paneer, cut into ¾-inch cubes

1 tablespoon unsalted butter

1 medium onion, chopped

1 bay leaf

1 (10-ounce) bag frozen peas

¾ cup buttermilk

½ cup roughly chopped fresh mint leaves

Zest and juice of 1 lemon

1 teaspoon kosher salt

White pepper

Heat a medium cast-iron or sauté pan over medium heat. Add the coconut oil and cook the paneer until crisp and browned on all sides, 2 to 3 minutes per side. Drain the cooked cheese on a plate lined with paper towels.

In the same pan over medium heat, melt the butter and sauté the onion and bay leaf until the onion is soft and translucent, about 3 minutes. Add the peas and buttermilk and cook until the peas are warmed through, about 5 minutes (the buttermilk will separate, but don't worry, it all comes together again in the food processor). Discard the bay leaf.

Pour the pea mixture into a food processor. Add the chopped mint, and the lemon zest and juice. Process for 1 minute, then season with the salt and white pepper. Process for 1 more minute. Return the pea mixture to the pan, nestle the paneer in the sauce, and gently reheat. Serve immediately with plenty of naan to sop up the extra sauce.

Serves 2 as an appetizer or 4 as a side dish, easy peas-y

Grilling Cheeses

A few more cheeses to sizzle, my nizzle.

NARRAGANSETT CREAMERY GRILLING CHEESE

Narragansett Creamery Grilling Cheese is a "Mediterranean-style" grilling cheese by way of Rhode Island that can be grilled or panfried. Think mild, slightly salty halloumi, but stateside.

PROVOLETA

Argentina has its own "sizzler," a provolone-style cheese called provoleta that's cooked on a grill or in a skillet and garnished with a flurry of fresh herbs. You can substitute provolone to similar effect, just ask your deli person to cut you a 1½-inch-thick slice. Because provolone has more moisture than provoleta, opt for a cast-iron or nonstick pan instead of the direct heat of a grill.

YANNI GRILLING CHEESE

If you're at a Walmart in the Midwest and craving some sizzle, keep an eye out for Yanni Grilling Cheese, a firm, salty cheese modeled after halloumi that's available in the most mainstream of markets.

BELGIOIOSO KASSERI

BelGioioso Kasseri, a dense, full-bodied cow's milk cheese that's quite sharp, can be eaten raw or cooked, a unique trait among sizzlers. It's modeled after Greek kasseri, a sheep's milk cheese sometimes used to make saganaki, the Greek flaming cheese dish. Kasseri won't take the direct heat of a grill, but it browns nicely in a cast-iron or nonstick pan.

GET WITH THE PAN
Why I Love Cast-Iron

Cast-iron is the Parmigiano Reggiano of cookware: It's good at one year, but you'll swear loyalty after two. It's one of the few pieces of kitchen equipment that truly gets better with age—my most treasured cast-iron pan is at least seventy years old (see Cheese Manicotti 4G, page 140). The cast-iron wares featured in this book are manufactured by Lodge, a Tennessee-based producer of affordable, high-quality cast-iron since 1910.

Properly seasoned and well-cared-for cast-iron is nonstick, a crucial requirement when cooking with cheese, as cheese that's been heated and cooled mimics glue. You could use a nonstick pan coated in polytetrafluoroethylene (aka Teflon), but there are valid concerns about its safety when it's heated too high or the coating deteriorates. Personally, I'd rather invest in an heirloom pan that lasts generations.

Cast-iron pans need a bit more time to preheat than most pans, but the extra time pays off: **cast-iron pans hold heat evenly and for a long time.** This is very helpful when cooking cheese, as it ensures an even melt and combats the great foe of good melt: temperature fluctuation.

Dip In

SHOW ME A DOWN-HOME GATHERING AND I'LL DIRECT YOU to the dip (and if I can't find a dip, then I'll direct you to a peeved auntie shouting, "Who forgot the dip?!"). There's a reason dips are the center of attention: they're the ultimate social food, a symbol of acceptance by the group.

Hot cheese dips are there for all those explorations of the human socio-culinary dynamic that are family gatherings—and for that needy bag of chips. Is that too much pressure to put on something as seemingly frivolous as a dip? Stay with me. (Think this ditty on the social dynamics of dip is ridic? Don't get me started on the stress test that is the last chip.)

The longer the cheese pull, the closer to God, and a bowl of bubbling hot curd raises the stakes in the dip drama. It's by far the most intense emotional roller coaster of dips. Not only are the thrills of the perfect bite that much more thrilling, but the disappointment when it's all over is a harder comedown, too.

The difference is urgency. Hot cheesy dips must be eaten immediately for optimal enjoyment, so nothing goes faster at a party. And with all this meaning floating in a bowl of hot cheese, it's imperative, for the host's own sanity, that hot cheese dips be a cinch to prepare. The torture of spending hours preparing something only to see it ravaged within a matter of minutes is too much for anyone to bear.

Baked Ricotta with Fresh Herbs

GET LIFTED

TRUSTED BRANDS: *BelGioioso, Calabro*

Ricotta (from the Latin *recocta*, "cooked twice") is traditionally made from whey, the liquid byproduct of coagulated milk. In the United States, most versions are made from whole cow's milk (you'll even find sheep's and goat's milk ricotta kicking around, though it's admittedly much less common). Feel free to use any type you come across for this soufflé-like dip, with plenty of crusty bread for dipping.

Unsalted butter for greasing

16 ounces ricotta (about 2 cups)

1 egg, lightly beaten

1 tablespoon grated lemon zest

1 tablespoon finely chopped flat-leaf parsley

1 teaspoon finely chopped chives

½ teaspoon finely chopped fresh oregano

½ teaspoon kosher salt

½ teaspoon crushed red pepper flakes

¼ teaspoon black pepper

5 basil leaves, finely chopped

Preheat the oven to 350°F. Butter a 16-ounce baking dish.

Mix all of the ingredients in a medium bowl, adding the basil last. Pour into the prepared dish and bake for 1 hour, until the ricotta puffs like a soufflé and is golden around the edges. Serve immediately.

Serves 6 for a cloud of cheesy goodness

Baked Feta with Pickled Peppers & Dill

GREEK DELIGHT

TRUSTED BRAND: *Mt Vikos*

This dip is a hot take on kopanisti, a classic Greek spread made with feta—a cheese that can be creamy and sweet with only a whisper of oceanic salinity, or compact, dry, and salty, like a mouthful of the Mediterranean. Feta is traditionally made of sheep's milk (think of the arid, craggy landscape of Greece; that's straight-up sheep country), though it's sometimes also made from a blend of sheep and goat's milk (goats like it craggy, too). It's then brined or packed in salt and aged anywhere from two to six months or longer. The addition of cottage cheese to this recipe makes this dip dippable, but do use the creamiest feta you can find. (If you're not sure which one that is, ask a cheesemonger for help.) The bright acidity and relatively gentle heat of the pickled peppers cut through the salty creaminess of the cheese. A generous portion of dill freshens it all up, and lemon zest draws out feta's natural citrus notes.

Unsalted butter for greasing

8 ounces feta, crumbled (2 cups)

8 ounces cottage cheese (1 cup)

2 pepperoncini, trimmed, deseeded, and finely chopped

2 peppadew peppers, finely chopped

1 garlic clove, minced

Zest and juice of 1 lemon

1 teaspoon dried oregano

½ teaspoon crushed red pepper flakes

½ cup chopped dill

Preheat the oven to 350°F. Butter a 16-ounce baking dish.

In a large bowl, thoroughly mix the feta and cottage cheese together. Add the rest of the ingredients and stir to combine.

Pour the mixture into the baking dish and tamp it down by gently banging the dish against the counter to settle the ingredients. Bake for 25 minutes, until the dip is golden around the edges and bubbling. Serve immediately, with warm pita for dipping.

Serves 6 to 8 for a taste of Greek life

Global Feta-ration

Although Greece will always own the cultural legacy that is feta cheese, countries around the world produce their own versions of this legendary cheese. Consider it proof of popularity rather than outright cultural appropriation; there's enough hunger for feta to support production in and outside of Greece. Over the years, heavy hitters have developed fetas with their own unique, delicious characteristics. Some of the most common:

ISRAELI FETA

Israeli feta most closely resembles the creamier types of Greek feta, though it tends to be less salty overall. This is an especially great style of feta for fruit salads.

AMERICAN FETA

American feta is typically mild, dry, and on the saltier side, making it an excellent candidate for crumbling into salads and using as a "finishing" cheese. It can be made from cow, sheep, or even goat's milk, though cow's milk is the most common.

FRENCH FETA

French feta is typically made from sheep's milk, and is a prudent choice when a cooked dish calls for a creamy, mild feta. This is my go-to for turning scrambled eggs into silky, cheesy goodness.

BULGARIAN FETA

Bulgarian feta is also typically made from sheep's milk, and is a bolder, saltier choice for cooking than French feta—especially if you like your cheese to have a whiff of animally funk (like I do!).

A Quick Recipe for Pita or Flatbread Chips

Pita (or flatbread) chips are sturdy enough to hold up to the heft and heat of hot cheese dips. They're certainly simple to make, and can be seasoned according to the needs of their betrothed dip. Pita, lavash, and naan are all good starting points—just remember to adjust the baking time according to the thickness of the bread.

Preheat the oven to 400°F. Line a baking sheet with parchment paper. Brush the parchment paper with 1 tablespoon olive oil and set aside.

Cut 4 pitas or flatbreads (such as lavash or naan) into quarters or eighths, depending on their size. If you're using pitas, split them in half around the pocket seam first.

Arrange the cut bread on the prepared baking sheet and brush with olive oil (you'll need 1 to 2 tablespoons).

Sprinkle the bread with salt and pepper and/or your choice of spice blend (curry powder, za'atar, or ras el hanout are obvious choices—but don't be afraid to make your own mix). Consider a simple dusting of salt, pepper, and lemon zest if you're making chips for Paneer in Minted Pea Sauce (see page 38), or salt and crushed red pepper flakes for chips to dip in Baked Ricotta with Fresh Herbs (see page 45). Dried dill and paprika are my choice for chips to accompany Baked Feta with Pickled Peppers & Dill (see page 46).

Bake in the oven for 5 minutes, then remove the pan from the oven, flip the chips, and continue to bake for 5 to 10 minutes, until golden brown (timing will depend on the thickness of the bread, and how dark you prefer your chips). Remove from the oven and cool completely before serving.

Makes 32 or so chips

Baked Pumpkin Fondue

MIDNIGHT SPECIAL

CHEESE OF CHOICE: *Any alpine or alpine-style cheese, such as Gruyère, Jasper Hill Farm Alpha Tolman, or Consider Bardwell Farm Rupert*

This autumn showstopper drops jaws for lunch, on a buffet, at a cocktail party, or as a communal starter. You could use a standard orange pumpkin here, but there's a better route if you've the option, a cheese pumpkin. Sweet, flavorful, and squat (don't hate; that makes it great for stuffing and dipping), the cheese pumpkin is an heirloom treasure indigenous to Long Island, so named because its color and proportions resemble a wheel (or tomme) of cheese. Similar recipes call for only heavy cream, but I like the way buttermilk (and lemon) play against the sweet flesh of the pumpkin and the savory meatiness of the cheese.

1 medium baguette, sliced into 1-inch-thick rounds

1 medium cheese pumpkin (about 5 pounds)

Kosher salt

Freshly ground black pepper

1 cup buttermilk

½ cup heavy cream

½ cup chicken or vegetable stock (homemade is best, or low-sodium store-bought)

1 tablespoon lemon zest

½ teaspoon dried thyme

¼ teaspoon freshly grated nutmeg

12 ounces cheese of choice, shredded (2½ cups)

1 tablespoon melted unsalted butter

Preheat the oven to 450°F. Toast the baguette slices on a large baking sheet in the oven, 5 to 7 minutes.

With a sharp pairing knife, cut a 4-inch circle around the stem of the pumpkin. Remove the top and clean the underside, scraping away any fibers and seeds. Clean the entire inside of the pumpkin (put the seeds aside to toast later, if inclined) and season with salt and freshly ground black pepper.

(continued)

In a medium bowl, whisk together the buttermilk, cream, stock, lemon zest, thyme, nutmeg, and ½ teaspoon salt and set aside.

Place a layer of toasted baguette slices in the bottom of the pumpkin, sprinkle 1 cup of the shredded cheese on top, then pour one-third of the buttermilk mixture on top of that. Repeat until the pumpkin is full (save any leftover toasted baguette for serving).

Brush a baking sheet and the exterior of the pumpkin with the melted butter. Bake for 1 hour, until the pumpkin is very tender and browned.

Serve it by scooping some of the fondue and pumpkin flesh onto a plate (this works for buffets) or slice the entire pumpkin like a pie (best for sit-down meals).

Serves 6 and does a disappearing act at midnight

Cheese Blends for Great Pumpkins

Looking beyond the Alps for cheeses to melt into a Baked Pumpkin Fondue.

MIXED MILKS

Different milks mean a broad range of flavors and textures. Consider Bardwell Farm Rupert, an alpine-style cow's milk cheese providing meltability and savory, grassy flavor; with Cypress Grove Lamb Chopper, a Gouda-style sheep's milk cheese that's sweet and nutty, and Vermont Creamery Chèvre, for tangy, grassy notes and creamy texture. *(Use a 3:2:1 ratio.)*

GO GOUDA

Mix different categories of Gouda to capture the sweet nuttiness (plus a little smoke) that's characteristic of the style. Marieke Golden, a young, buttery, semi-soft cow's milk Gouda for easy melting; plus Maple Leaf Smoked Gouda, a hickory-smoked cow's milk Gouda for meaty smokiness; and Marieke Aged Gouda, aged 9 to 12 months, for sweet caramel notes. *(Use a 2:1:1 ratio.)*

UMAMI IT UP

Harness the rich, complex flavors of truffles and blue cheese. Fontina, a mild cow's milk cheese that's oh-so-melty; Grafton Truffle Cheddar Bar, a nutty Vermont cheddar with the dank earthiness of Italian truffles; and Gorgonzola Cremificato, an übercreamy mild blue cheese that's almost sweet. *(Use a 3:2:1 ratio.)*

Baked Brie Kataifi with Honey

RELIGIOUS EXPERIENCE

TRUSTED BRAND: *Marin French Cheese Company*

Once I made baked Brie with kataifi instead of the traditional puff pastry, I never looked back. Kataifi is a prepared dough found at all Greek and Middle Eastern specialty food stores. It's like a shredded phyllo dough, but much easier to work with than either phyllo or puff pastry. It has no propensity to sog and its default is crispy, returning more crunch per square inch than poor, pallid puff. A drizzle of good honey sweetens the deal.

2 tablespoons melted unsalted butter

1 (6 to 8 ounce) Brie

6 ounces kataifi

¼ cup honey

Preheat the oven to 425°F.

Brush a pie plate with a teaspoon of the melted butter. Place the Brie in the center of the plate.

Divide the kataifi into three strands and braid the strands together. Place the braid around the cheese, surrounding it like a wreath or nest, then brush the kataifi with the remaining melted butter.

Bake 15 to 20 minutes, until the kataifi is deeply golden and crispy. Drizzle with the honey and serve immediately.

Serves 4 as an appetizer or 2 as foreplay

Get Bloomy & Baked

Many small-format, bloomy-rind cheeses are transformed into pure, unadulterated cheese dip when baked in a 350°F oven. Place a room temperature cheese on a baking sheet lined with parchment paper and bake 10 to 12 minutes, until the cheese swells like a belly full of butterfat (don't worry, it's just the paste of the cheese expanding as it heats). Keep a close eye on the cheese while it bakes—you don't want it to bust through the rind while cooking. Here are a few bakeable bloomies, with pairings to sweeten the deal:

COWGIRL CREAMERY MT TAM

Cowgirl Creamery Mt Tam is a dense cow's milk triple-cream bomb from California that's perfect for two. Jammit Jam Apple Cinnamon Bourbon Whole Fruit Spread has a hint of booze to cut through the fat. *(Serves 2 to 4)*

SWEET GRASS DAIRY GREEN HILL

Sweet Grass Dairy Green Hill is a buttery puck of cow's milk from Georgia that's all sunshine, hay, and hallelujah. Lemon Bird Preserves Cantaloupe with Vanilla Bean Jam keeps it bright. *(Serves 2 to 4)*

MT. TOWNSEND CREAMERY CIRRUS

Mt. Townsend Creamery Cirrus is a Camembert-inspired round of buttery, nutty, creamy cow's milk deliciousness. Gus & Grey Notorious FIG brandied fig jam matches the rich depth of the cheese bite for bite. *(Serves 2 to 4)*

JASPER HILL FARM MOSES SLEEPER

Jasper Hill Farm Moses Sleeper is a direct descendent of Brie, by way of Vermont. Notes of crème fraîche and fresh hazelnuts make this creamy wheel a tart and nutty bake. Brin's Jam & Marmalade Lemon Poppyseed Marmalade reinforces the vibe. *(Serves 6 to 8)*

SPOON CHEESES

Dip Right In

Without heat, these "spoon cheeses" (more suited to a spoon than a knife) are totally dip-worthy. But hit them with some heat (see Get Bloomy & Baked, opposite) and they transform from really good to absolutely glorious. (Can you hear the angels singing?)

VERMONT CREAMERY ST. ALBANS

Vermont Creamery St. Albans comes in its own crock and liquefies into a rich and tangy quickie fondue. Quince & Apple Shallot Confit with Red Wine answers that tang.

JASPER HILL FARM HARBISON

Jasper Hill Farm Harbison is girdled in spruce bark, influsing it with the woodsy, forest-floor notes of the Vermont landscape. INNA jam Apricot Chutney with ginger and coriander brings out the meaty aspect of this rustic puck.

UPLANDS CHEESE COMPANY RUSH CREEK RESERVE

Rush Creek Reserve is made every fall in Wisconsin, and it's worth the wait for the rich, puddingy paste ripe with toasted hay and brothy flavors. Jammy Yummy Baby Portobello Jam reinforces the earthy, savory notes of the cheese.

Goat Cheese Queso Fundido

HOT SKILLET

TRUSTED BRAND: *Montchevre*

There are fundido recipes that call for a fondue-like technique, where the cheese is emulsified into liquid, but I like to focus my cooking on the veggie and meat base, and just melting a boat-load of cheese over it. Goat's milk cheddar is the foundation here, with a flex of bright, tangy, jalapeño-flecked chèvre. Goat's milk cheeses give the fundido a brightness that quells the heat of the chorizo and jalapeño. A finishing flourish of goat's milk feta acts as finishing salt.

1 tablespoon olive oil

½ cup diced yellow onion

½ cup diced red bell pepper

1 jalapeño, diced (if you prefer less heat discard the seeds)

1 garlic clove, minced

⅛ teaspoon ground cumin

1 cup diced cured chorizo

8 ounces goat's milk cheddar, shredded (2 cups)

2 ounces jalapeño goat's milk chèvre, crumbled (¼ cup)

2 ounces goat's milk feta, crumbled (¼ cup)

2 scallions, chopped

¼ cup chopped cilantro

Tortilla chips for serving

Position a rack in the upper third of the oven and preheat the broiler.

Heat the olive oil in a medium cast-iron or sauté pan over medium heat. Sauté the onion until translucent, about 3 minutes. Add the pepper, jalapeño, garlic, and cumin and sauté until the vegetables are soft, about 2 minutes. Add the chorizo and mix in the cheddar, then dot with the chèvre and feta.

Transfer the skillet to the oven and broil for 7 minutes, until the fundido is melted and just starting to brown on top. Sprinkle with the scallion and cilantro and serve immediately, with warm tortilla chips.

Serves 4 for goaty gloriousness

THERE'S NOTHING QUITE LIKE THE SENSORIAL ROLLER COASTER of butterfat cooked in more fat. Crispy, crunchy, silky, and oozy is one helluva foursome. And it all comes down to the fat. Fat, fat, fat . . . did I say fat? Now that the fat's out of the bag, shall we proceed? Clearly, fried cheese isn't a health food, and it definitely shouldn't be eaten every day, but that doesn't mean it deserves total banishment. As an occasional treat, fried cheese can't be beat.

When deep-frying, it's crucial to get the oil temperature where it needs to be and then to hold it there. Fry in tepid oil and you'll end up with a spongy mess. Fry in oil that's too hot and your end result will be burnt on the outside and undercooked on the inside. (Crispy and cold is the cruelest cheese tease.) A frying thermometer is a good precaution against flubbing the oil temp; there's really no reason not to use one.

Small batches are also key. Don't crowd the oil! The fewer pieces fried at a time, the less the oil temperature fluctuates. Draining is important, because oily fried cheese is truly, inarguably, unequivocally disgusting. Some foods can be fried ahead of time and kept waiting in an oven until they're ready to serve. Cheese is not one of them. Never hold and reheat fried cheese.

Lastly, fried cheese loves acidity. A lashing of something bright brings focus to the fat. Peppy sauces, perky chutneys, and pops of acid-tinged flavors (or even just a squeeze of lemon) take fried cheese from flabby to fierce.

Fried Burrata with Roasted Tomatoes

CRISPY CLOUD

TRUSTED BRAND: *BelGioioso*

Sure, there's a time and a place for fried mozzarella sticks, but that time is not now. Dress a milky orb of burrata in crispy fried breadcrumbs, surround it with a moat of juicy, tangy roasted tomatoes, and you've got a virtual stairway to heaven. A wee bit of whey will leak from the burrata while frying—don't worry, they're tears of joy.

1 (8-ounce) burrata

1 pint cherry tomatoes

4 garlic cloves, minced

2 tablespoons balsamic vinegar

1 tablespoon olive oil

1 teaspoon kosher salt

4 sprigs fresh thyme

Handful of fresh basil leaves

Freshly ground black pepper

Frying oil (see A Quick Guide to Frying Oils, page 80)

1 egg

½ cup heavy cream

½ cup all-purpose flour

1 cup panko breadcrumbs

½ teaspoon dried oregano

Preheat the oven to 425°F. Remove the burrata from the refrigerator and drain it on paper towels.

Line a baking sheet with parchment paper or a silicone baking mat. In a medium bowl, toss the tomatoes, garlic, vinegar, olive oil, ½ teaspoon salt, thyme, basil, and black pepper. Spread the mixture onto the baking sheet and bake for 15 minutes, until the garlicky smell of the tomatoes beckons you to the oven, and the tomatoes are browned in a few spots and bursting. Remove the tomatoes from the oven, discard the thyme sprigs, and set aside. Lower the oven to 350°F.

(continued)

Pour the oil into a deep heavy-bottomed pan to a depth of 4 inches. Heat on medium to 375°F. Line a small baking dish with paper towels.

In a wide, shallow bowl, beat the egg and cream together. Place the flour in a separate wide, shallow bowl. Mix the breadcrumbs, oregano, and the remaining ½ teaspoon salt together in a third shallow bowl. Gently coat the burrata in flour, then place it in the bowl with the egg mixture. Baste it with a spoon so it's completely coated in the egg mixture, then place it in the breadcrumbs and roll gently to coat completely. Repeat the last two steps for a second coating in the egg mixture and then the breadcrumbs.

With a spider or slotted spoon, slowly lower the burrata into the hot oil. Fry, turning once, until dark golden brown, 5 to 7 minutes. Transfer the fried burrata to the prepared dish to drain, then remove the paper towels and place it in the oven. Put the tomatoes back in the same oven to reheat.

Bake until the cheese is molten in the center, about 10 minutes. Remove the burrata and the tomatoes from the oven.

Place the burrata in a wide, shallow bowl or wide platter. Spoon the warm roasted tomatoes around it and serve immediately, with toasted country bread—or garlic bread, if you're extra.

Serves 4 for an orgiastic appetizer

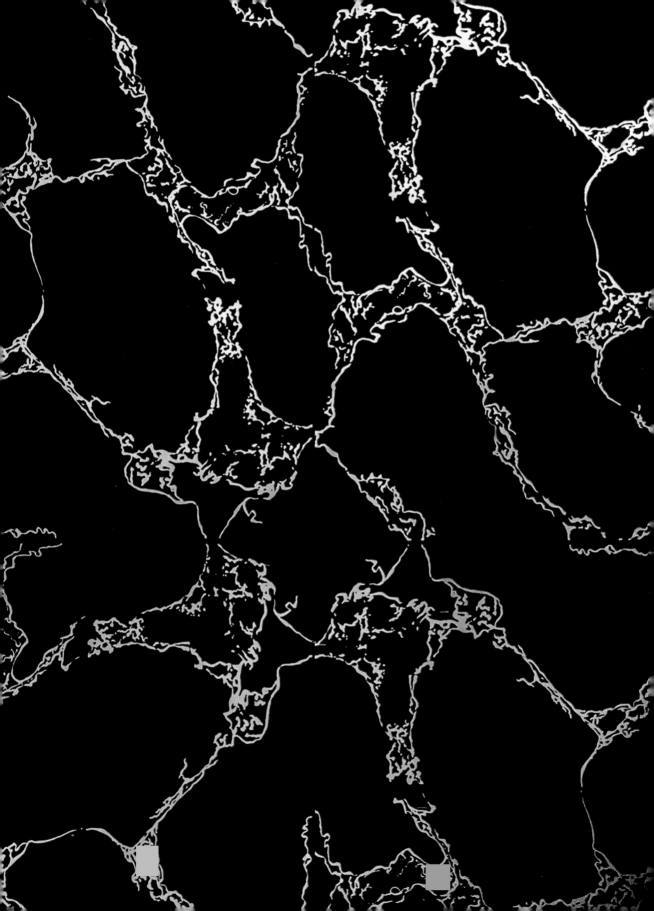

Fried Chèvre

STILL CRAZY AFTER ALL THESE YEARS

TRUSTED BRANDS: *Montchevre, Vermont Creamery, Laura Chenel*

Channel your inner 1980s caterer with fried goat cheese, but keep it relevant with a zippy parsley sauce that plays against the rich tang of goat's milk. In general, knowing how to expertly fry goat cheese is a nice little back-pocket skill. It's delicious on its own with any number of sauces, and can take a salad from "I threw this together" to totally bitchin'.

1 (8-ounce) log of chèvre

1 cup panko breadcrumbs

1 teaspoon kosher salt

½ teaspoon sweet paprika

½ teaspoon freshly ground black pepper

2 eggs

¼ cup all-purpose flour

Frying oil (see A Quick Guide to Frying Oils, page 80)

Place the chèvre in the freezer for 10 minutes, to make it easier to cut, then slice it crosswise into 8 equal-sized disks.

Cover a large plate with parchment paper. In a small shallow bowl, combine the panko, salt, paprika, and pepper. In a second bowl, beat the eggs. Place the flour in a third bowl. Working with one piece of chèvre at a time, lightly coat it in flour, shaking off any excess. Dredge it in the egg, coating completely and holding the cheese over the bowl for a few seconds to allow the excess egg to drip off. Transfer it to the breadcrumb mixture and spoon the breadcrumbs over it or very gently toss it to coat the cheese completely. Place the cheese on the parchment-lined plate and repeat with the remaining pieces. Put the plate in the freezer and chill the breaded cheese for 15 minutes before frying.

Pour the oil into a cast-iron or heavy-bottomed pan to a depth of 1 inch. Heat on medium to 350°F. Heat the oven to 250°F. Remove the breaded cheese from the freezer and fry in batches, turning once, until golden brown on both sides, 5 to 7 minutes. Drain on paper towels, then place on a baking sheet and hold in a warm oven until all of the cheese is fried. Serve immediately with sauce on the side.

Serves 4 people with self-control or 2 without

Quick Parsley Sauce

In a food processor fitted with a blade attachment, combine 1 chopped garlic clove, 1 large, roughly chopped bunch of parsley (leaves and stems), the zest and juice of 1 lemon, 1 teaspoon kosher salt, ½ teaspoon crushed red pepper flakes, and ¼ teaspoon freshly ground black pepper. Pulse until very fine.

With the food processor still running, add ¼ cup water and 2 tablespoons maple syrup, then slowly add ½ cup of the best extra virgin olive oil you have and pulse until very smooth. *Makes 1 cup.*

Use it as a dipping sauce for the fried goat cheese, or drizzle it over the top of the cheese. It also works well drizzled on Fried Burrata with Roasted Tomatoes (see page 62) as an additional layer of flavor.

OR, JUST BUY THIS

Friend in Cheeses Jam Co. Salted Watermelon Jelly

Watermelon and goat cheese are always a good match, and this jelly, inspired by sticky summer nights on the porch, is a fun cooldown for hot fried chèvre.

A Year of Fried Chèvre Salads

Now that you know how to transform a creamy log of chèvre into crispy coins of deliciousness, it's time to pay it forward with salads. Fried chèvre adds protein and main-meal heft, but, perhaps more meaningfully, it makes salads special enough to be company-worthy. Springtime is the traditional season for chèvre, but fried chèvre knows no season: it's great year-round, with spring salads of tender greens or hearty winter salads with roasted root vegetables. Served for lunch or brunch, they're light on time and a heavy-on-pizzazz choice for entertaining, no matter the season.

SPRING

Fried chèvre over Little Gem or baby romaine lettuce, with tarragon, shaved fennel, and thinly sliced strawberries, dressed with sherry vinegar, olive oil, salt, and pepper

SUMMER

Fried chèvre over butter or Bibb lettuce, with tomatoes, thinly sliced radishes, and crumbled bacon, dressed with white wine vinegar, olive oil, salt, and pepper

FALL

Fried chèvre over kale or arugula, with roasted squash, Nicoise olives, and toasted pumpkin seeds, dressed with lemon juice, olive oil, salt, and pepper

WINTER

Fried chèvre over escarole or watercress, with pomegranate arils, pears, pickled onions, and spiced pecans, dressed with red wine vinegar, olive oil, salt, and pepper

Fried Cheese Curds

WISCONSIN CAVIAR

TRUSTED BRANDS: *see Cheddar, Interrupted, page 81*

No one does the cheese lifestyle quite like Wisconsin, which makes more than 2.5 billion pounds of cheese a year, more than any other state. Residents of "America's Dairyland" proudly call themselves cheeseheads, and one of their most important contributions to the industry are cheese curds, or "squeaky cheese," named because of the sound they make when chewed. Cheese curds come from Wisconsin because a ton of cheddar is produced there; in fact, they're part of the cheddar-making process—what cheddar is before being pressed into wheels and aged. When fried, they're squeaky and crunchy, and a perfect little vessel for any number of condiments.

Frying oil (see A Quick Guide to Frying Oils, page 80)

1 pound cheese curds

½ cup cornstarch

1 cup all-purpose flour

1½ teaspoons baking powder

½ teaspoon kosher salt

1 (12-ounce) bottle lager beer

Pour the oil into a heavy-bottomed pan with high sides to a depth of 3 inches. Heat on medium to 350°F.

In a medium bowl, toss the cheese curds in the cornstarch. In a large bowl whisk together the flour, baking powder, and salt, then slowly whisk in the beer, mixing until the batter is lump-free. The batter should be thin and foamy.

Scoop the cheese curds from the cornstarch with a slotted spoon, shaking the spoon to remove any excess. Quickly dip the spoon with the curds into the batter to coat, then hold the spoon over the bowl to let excess batter drip off. Gingerly drop the battered cheese curds into the oil by hand one at a time, frying in batches of up to a dozen curds. Turn the curds as they fry, until they're deep golden brown, 5 to 6 minutes. Drain on paper towels and serve immediately with a zippy sauce.

Serves 4 for squeaky fried fun

Buffalo Curds with Blue Cheese Dip

In a medium bowl, combine ½ cup sour cream, ½ cup crème fraîche, and ¼ teaspoon each Old Bay seasoning, celery seed, and white pepper.

Add 4 ounces crumbled blue cheese, mix thoroughly, adjust seasonings if needed, and place in a small serving bowl.

In a large bowl, whisk together 4 tablespoons hot sauce (I prefer Frank's Red Hot) with 4 tablespoons melted unsalted butter.

Fry and drain the cheese curds, then gently toss them in the hot sauce–butter mixture.

Serve immediately, with blue cheese dip and celery and carrot sticks on the side.

New York Shuk Harissa with Preserved Lemon

Sun-dried chile peppers and a secret spice blend make this flavorful and not-too-spicy staple of North African cooking a ketchup-meets-Sriracha condiment. This version, made by a wife-and-husband culinary team based in New York City, harnesses the floral brightness of preserved lemon, a serious amount of garlic, and toasted caraway to perk up the subtle heat of the chile peppers. Paired with hot, crispy curds, it's a real humdinger.

Little Dutch Eggs

YOU'RE WELCOME

RECOMMENDED: *young Gouda*
TRUSTED BRAND: *Marieke Gouda*

This riff on Scotch eggs replaces the traditional ground meat with "Dutch gold," (aka Gouda) for a meltingly transgressive hot cheese snack. These little parcels of gooey cheese and egg can be prepped ahead of time and popped in the fryer when the party feels ready for its hot cheese moment. Refrigerate them in the meantime, but remember to pop them in the freezer for 15 minutes before cooking to keep them from leaking cheese while they're in the fryer.

10 ounces young Gouda, shredded (about 2¼ cups)

2 tablespoons cornstarch

½ teaspoon mustard powder

½ teaspoon Old Bay seasoning

½ teaspoon kosher salt

¼ teaspoon freshly ground black pepper

½ cup finely chopped parsley

1 tablespoon Worcestershire sauce

3 tablespoons lager beer

4 hard-boiled eggs, peeled, plus 2 raw eggs

½ cup all-purpose flour

½ cup heavy cream

1 cup panko breadcrumbs

Frying oil (see A Quick Guide to Frying Oils, page 80)

Put the cheese, cornstarch, mustard powder, Old Bay, salt, pepper, and parsley in the bowl of a food processor fitted with the blade attachment and pulse to combine. Add the Worcestershire and beer and process until the mixture is very smooth.

Gather a heaping tablespoon of the cheese mixture, roll it into a ball, then pat it between both hands into a pancake. Place a hard-boiled egg in the center of the cheese, then mold it around the egg. Repeat with the remaining 3 hard-boiled eggs.

(continued)

Place the flour in a wide, shallow bowl. In a second bowl, beat the 2 eggs and cream together. Place the breadcrumbs in a third wide, shallow bowl. Lightly roll each wrapped egg in the flour to coat and transfer it to the bowl with the egg mixture. Baste it with a spoon so it's completely coated in liquid, then transfer it to the bowl with the breadcrumbs. Spoon breadcrumbs over and press lightly to coat each completely. Repeat the last two steps, basting with the egg mixture and coating with the breadcrumbs, with each egg. Transfer the breaded eggs to a plate lined with parchment paper and chill, uncovered, for 15 minutes in the freezer.

Pour the oil into a heavy-bottomed pan with high sides to a depth of 4 inches. Heat on medium to 375°F. Remove the eggs from the freezer and fry 2 at a time until deep golden, about 6 minutes. Place on paper towels to drain for 1 minute and serve immediately.

Serves 4 peckish guests as an appetizer

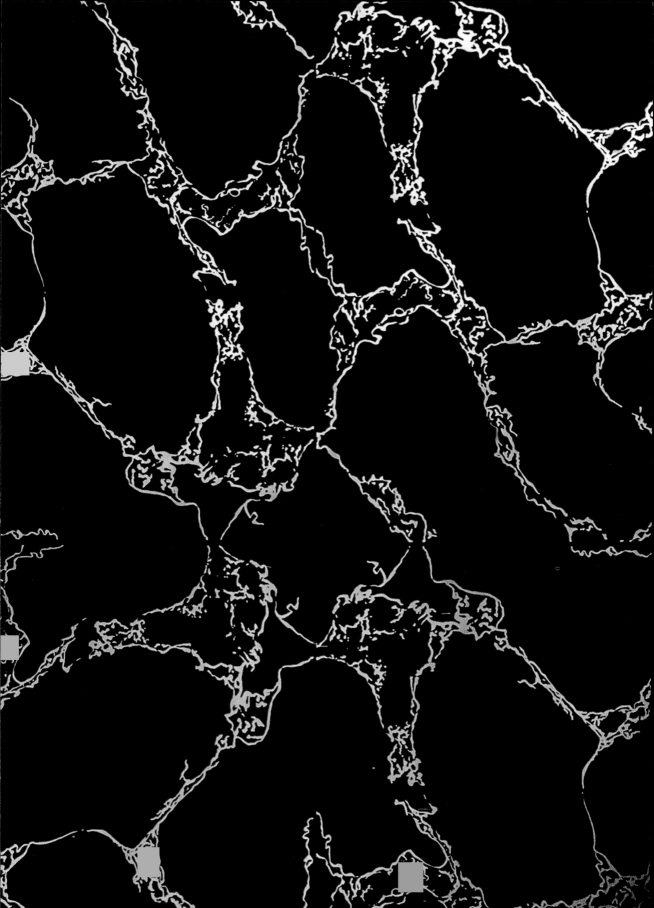

Malakoff

HOT CHEESE WORTH FIGHTING FOR

TRADITIONAL: *Gruyère*

SUBSTITUTIONS: *Any firm alpine or alpine-style cheese, such as Saxon Creamery Saxony Alpine Style or Consider Bardwell Farm Rupert*

A Malakoff is a fondue in fried form: Gruyère bound with cornstarch, moistened with wine, and seasoned with nutmeg is molded atop a slice of baguette then fried and served with mustard and cornichons on the side. Its name honors a siege during the Crimean War of 1855, when Swiss mercenaries captured the Malakoff Tower in what is now Ukraine. Apparently hot cheese can be a battle cry.

1 pound Gruyère, shredded (about 4 cups)

2 tablespoons cornstarch

1 teaspoon kosher salt

½ teaspoon onion powder

½ teaspoon white pepper

¼ teaspoon freshly grated nutmeg

2 eggs

¼ cup dry white wine

12 (½-inch-thick) slices of baguette

Frying oil (see A Quick Guide to Frying Oils, page 80)

Mustard and cornichons, for serving

In the bowl of a food processor fitted with the blade attachment, combine the Gruyère with the cornstarch, salt, onion powder, white pepper, nutmeg, eggs, and white wine. Process until the mixture is very smooth and sticks together when pinched. If it's too dry, add a bit more wine.

Line a baking sheet with parchment paper. With a spoon or sandwich spreader, scoop up a heaping tablespoon of the cheese mixture and mold it onto one side of a baguette slice, shaping it into a hill-like slope. Smooth the seam where the cheese and bread meet and place on the prepared baking sheet. Repeat until all of the cheese mixture is used, then freeze the Malakoffs for 30 minutes.

Pour the oil into a heavy-bottomed pan with high sides to a depth of 4 inches. Heat on medium to 375°F. Fry the Malakoffs, cheese side down, in batches of 4, until pale golden brown, 3 to 4 minutes. Turn and fry on the other side until golden, about 2 more minutes. Drain on paper towels and serve immediately with mustard and cornichons on the side. Malakoffs can be eaten with a fork and knife, or with fingers.

Makes 12 mighty Malakoffs for a small army of 4 to 6

A QUICK GUIDE TO FRYING OILS
TGI Fry Day

When choosing frying oil, flavor and smoke point (the temperature at which a particular oil starts to burn) are your top considerations. For the deep-frying recommended in this chapter, choose a neutral oil with a smoke point over 400°F.

PEANUT OIL

Peanut oil that has been refined is for frying; unrefined peanut oil is a salad or finishing oil. A high smoke point (450°F) means it's a good, forgiving choice when it comes to temperature maintenance, though it's obviously off-limits for folks with peanut allergies.

VEGETABLE OIL

Vegetable oil is a mysterious blend of plant-based oils that are most likely not very good for you, with a smoke point of 400° to 450°F, depending on the blend. Still, it's a ubiquitous workhorse, inexpensive, and was probably your grandma's favorite.

CANOLA OIL

Canola oil doesn't smoke until it's heated to 450°F. A bit pricier than peanut or vegetable oil, it's a good choice if you're looking to avoid peanuts, but don't want to go rogue with vegetable oil.

Cheddar, Interrupted

Cheese curds are a step in the cheddar-making process, interrupted: they're curds that haven't yet been pressed into the molds that could turn them into a wheel of cheddar cheese. They're primarily (though not exclusively) found in cheddar-producing regions—most famously Wisconsin and Quebec. Depending on where you live, you can score cheese curds at supermarkets, farmer's markets, specialty food stores, cheese shops, or directly from cheese makers online. The best curds are the freshest curds, so choose a supplier with good turnaround. Some reliable producers of American curds:

CARR VALLEY CHEESE COMPANY

ROELLI CHEESE HAUS

ELLSWORTH COOPERATIVE CREAMERY
(check out the Hot Buffalo and Garlic flavors)

MAPLEBROOK FARM
(they call them "cheddar bites")

BIRCHRUN HILLS FARM

BEEHIVE CHEESE CO.
(check out the Squeaky Bee Ragin' Cajun and Smokey Jalapeno flavors)

BEECHER'S HANDMADE CHEESE

Sandwhatevers

SANDWICHES ARE THE ORIGINAL CONVENIENCE FOOD, AND AN easy and versatile way to get in a dose of hot cheese, coming together with a just few ingredients or building out into elaborate knife-and-fork affairs. The flexibility of cheese and bread (or something bread-like) are a canvas for all kinds of exploration, and most cultures with a cheese tradition have some kind of sandwich tradition, too.

This chapter combines sandwiches with other less easily defined cheese and carb flirtations, what you might call "sandwhatevers." Generally, what links the recipes is they're eaten casually and cheese is crucial to their comportment. Cheese may not be the main ingredient in a pljeskavica—a cheese-stuffed burger from the Balkans—for instance, but it wouldn't be one without it (without it, it'd be just a burger, instead of the messy, cheesy surprise party that it is).

Let's talk about grilled cheese. There are entire books dedicated to this iconic comfort food, with myriad variations on the theme, and everyone has a personal favorite. I haven't tried to define the ultimate version here, instead offering straightforward tips on the hows and whys of a perfectly grilled cheese, including some that you may not have considered before. A great grilled cheese needs a thoughtful approach more than obedience to a "master recipe," but I've included a pretty foolproof one here. Use it as a way to master the fundamentals and tailor to your own taste.

Above all, I encourage you to develop an appreciation for the comingling of bread and cheese as a universal construct of on-the-go deliciousness. One man's grilled cheese is another man's khachipuri, because even though it may not be a slice of American toasted on white bread, it shares the same spirit.

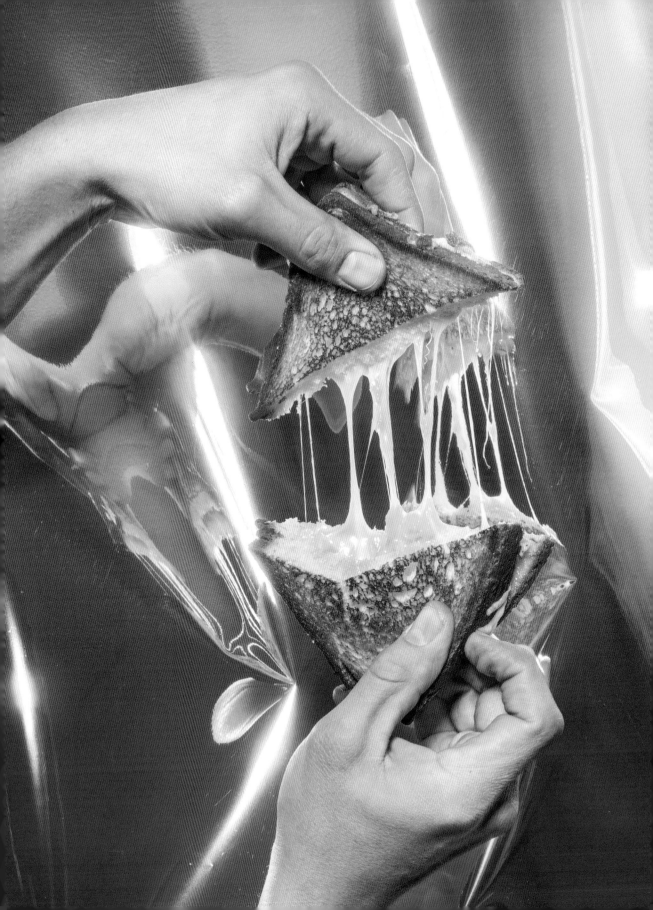

American-Style Grilled Cheese

THIS RULES

Few things are more satisfying than a grilled cheese. For many it can be a lifelong love affair, an unmitigated communion of desire—bread, heat, and cheese—no utensils required. Objectively, there's no single way to make a great grilled cheese, but I have my preferred method derived from a career making thousands.

2 teaspoons clarified butter

2 (½-inch-thick) slices wheat bread

2 ounces each young cheddar and Monterey Jack, shredded

Preheat the oven to 300°F, and set a wire rack in a baking sheet. Heat a cast-iron skillet over low heat.

Spread ½ teaspoon clarified butter on one side of each slice of bread. Add 1 teaspoon clarified butter to the pan. Once it's melted, increase the heat to medium and add the first slice of bread, buttered side down, to the pan. Working quickly, mound the cheese evenly in the center of the bread, leaving a half-inch border on all sides. Top with the second slice, buttered side up, and gently press down. Cook until the bottom slice is evenly golden brown, then carefully flip the sandwich and cook the other side until toasted and golden.

Transfer to the wire rack and place in the oven to finish melting or to keep hot while you cook another one. When ready to eat, remove the finished grilled cheese from the oven, let rest for 1 minute on a cutting board, and slice diagonally. Serve immediately.

Makes 1 perfect grilled cheese

Grilled Cheese How-to

THE CHEESE

Barring processed cheese, the go-to cheeses for a typical American grilled cheese are cheddar, Monterey Jack, or (and this is a more recent development) alpine and alpine-style cheeses, such as Gruyère. I fully support the use of any of these, though I have a personal preference for a mix of cheddar and Monterey Jack: the first for flavor, the second for meltability.

Whatever kind of cheese I'm using, and whatever kind of grilled cheese I'm making, I always shred my cheese (unless I'm using presliced cheese). Shredding helps the cheese melt faster and more evenly. If that seems like too much work, break up sliced cheese into smaller pieces. Whatever you do, don't succumb to the postmodern hell of preshredded cheese. It's coated in mystery starch and doesn't taste nearly as good as when you shred it yourself.

THE BREAD

An ideal choice for grilled cheese is a bread with some structure that's not too crusty. Soft, ultraprocessed supermarket bread is too flimsy, but a crusty baguette will tear up your mouth once toasted. Lately I've noticed a spike in the use of fruit and nut breads, but I personally don't understand this particular form of madness. A medium-crumbed sandwich bread, white or whole wheat, perhaps just flirting with staleness, is tops. A sturdy bread provides a structurally sound base for the cheese, holding up the fat and heat treatment of a grilled cheese. Very soft, processed white (think Wonder Bread) or even brioche just doesn't deliver the crunch to contrast with the ooze of hot cheese. I always buy unsliced bread when possible, and prefer a slightly thicker slice for a grilled cheese than the standard thickness of presliced bread.

THE FAT

Clarified butter is your friend. It has a higher smoke point than standard butter, but still lends the sweet richness that plays an important supporting role in the flavor of a grilled cheese. Spread it on the bread, then add some to the hot pan before cooking each grilled cheese. If you can't be bothered to clarify butter (and that's valid), use regular butter, but watch the heat closely so it doesn't burn.

THE HEAT

Getting the perfect combination of toasted bread and melted cheese is an easy two-step process. Preheat the oven to 300°F and preheat your skillet over medium-low heat as you shred the cheese and butter the bread. This simple step is crucial to achieving a pan that is heated evenly. Increase the heat to medium just before adding the bread to the pan. Once toasted, transfer your grilled cheese to the oven for about two minutes (or until the remaining grilled cheese sandwiches are toasted). The gentle oven heat gets the cheese over the melt finish line without burning the bread, and will keep the first ones hot if you're cooking more than one. Cut each grilled cheese in half only once you're ready to eat them (and diagonally, always diagonally to glorify the cheese melt).

BuffArepa
STREET DECADENCE

RECOMMENDED: *mozzarella di bufala DOP, BelGioioso fresh mozzarella*

A "BuffArepa" is a homemade version of a MozzArepa®, the buttery, sweet corn pancakes and gooey melted mozzarella that are a staple of New York City street fairs. Here, I've swapped the filling of regular ol' mozzarella cheese for creamier, slightly sweeter mozzarella di bufala, made from water buffalo's milk, which is even more decadent than the traditional version made from cow's milk. The batter also contains mozzarella, but no need to switch it up there, just make sure to use full-fat (not "part-skim"). Masarepa, a precooked ground cornmeal, can be found at most supermarkets with a Latin food section (Goya brand is trustworthy).

2 cups whole milk

4 tablespoons (½ stick) unsalted butter, cubed

2 tablespoons honey

1½ cups yellow masarepa

2 tablespoons sugar

2 teaspoons kosher salt

4 ounces whole milk mozzarella, shredded (about 1 cup)

½ cup fresh corn kernels, cut from the cob (about 1 ear)

2 tablespoons canola or peanut oil

1 (8-ounce) ball mozzarella di bufala, cut into ½-inch-thick slices

Preheat the oven to 350°F.

Set a small saucepan with the milk over medium-high heat. As soon as the milk comes to a boil, remove the pan from the heat and whisk in the butter and honey until melted. Cover to keep warm and set aside.

In a large bowl, stir together the masarepa, sugar, salt, shredded cheese, and corn. Make a well in the center and pour in about 1½ cups of the milk mixture. Stir the mixture with a fork until completely blended and no dry lumps remain.

(continued)

With your hands, knead the mixture in the bowl, adding the remaining milk mixture 1 tablespoon at a time as necessary until the dough is smooth and very sticky. You may not use all of the milk mixture; stir any leftovers into tea or coffee.

Place the dough in the center of a long sheet of parchment paper, top with another sheet, and carefully roll out into a rectangle with a ¾-inch thickness. Cut into 3-inch-diameter circles with a biscuit or cookie cutter or a juice glass. Reroll the scraps as needed to get 16 uniform circles.

Preheat a large cast-iron griddle or pan over medium-low heat for 5 minutes. Brush the pan with some of the oil. Cook the arepas in batches until they brown, about 4 minutes on each side. Transfer to a plate to cool, until you're ready to fill them.

Sandwich slices of the mozzarella di bufala between the browned arepas and place on a baking sheet lined with parchment paper. Set in the oven and bake about 4 minutes, until the mozzarella di bufala is melted. Serve immediately, slathered with a pat of buffalo milk butter, if you're feeling decadent (this product is available at large retailers, or look for it online).

Makes 8 BuffArepas, which will satisfy 4 to 6 for a filling snack

For a Truly Great Grilled Cheese, Mix It Up!

Why choose one cheese when you can have two? Shredding and blending cheeses lets you home in on a more precise flavor and melt for your grilled cheese.

CHEDDAR

Cheddar brings the savory, tangy flavor (and annatto-orange color) you've come to expect in a classic American grilled cheese, but Monterey Jack, with its mild flavor and smooth melting moves, ensures you'll get that dramatic stretch-and-pull. *(Use a 1:1 ratio.)*

GRUYÈRE

Gruyère is a sophisticated choice for a grilled cheese: it has a more complex arch of flavors (think beef broth, caramelized onions, and brown butter) than most grilled cheese go-tos. But mild Emmentaler has the meltability that'll hold a GC together, without interfering with the flavor multitudes brought by Gruyère. *(Use a 2:1 ratio.)*

SMOKED GOUDA

On its own, smoked Gouda is too smoky for me to commit to in a grilled cheese. You can adjust the smoke level by cutting in some Havarti, which melts beautifully. Think campfire, not dumpster fire. *(Go with your palate for these ratios.)*

FONTINA

Fontina is famous for its melt, but flavorwise it can fall flat—especially more generic supermarket styles. Aged Asiago adds a Parm-like tang that also contributes a bit of texture, as it won't melt fully into the fontina. *(My recommended ratio is 3:1.)*

Pljeskavica

STUFFED BALKAN BURGER

Pljeskavica is a hamburger-like dish found throughout the former Yugoslavia, primarily in Serbia, Croatia, Bosnia and Herzegovina, and Montenegro. There, every region (more realistically, every cook) has its own special recipe, with different blends of meat (beef, veal, pork, and/or lamb), spices, and fillings, though paprika and minced onions are standard. The meat patty is then stuffed with cheese, usually a briny, young sheep's milk cheese—a staple in Balkan cuisine—and grilled. Traditionally, pljeskavica is served in lepinja, a fluffy pita-style flatbread, with salata (pickled salad), kaymak (a fermented dairy spread similar to clotted cream), and ajvar (roasted red pepper spread), though you'd be cool to go with pita, pickles, sour cream, and roasted red peppers here.

1 pound lean ground beef

1 pound ground lamb

¼ cup minced onion

1 teaspoon sweet paprika

½ teaspoon garlic powder

½ teaspoon kosher salt

½ teaspoon freshly ground black pepper

2 ounces creamy feta, crumbled (about ¼ cup) (see Global Feta-ration, page 48)

4 ounces whole milk mozzarella, shredded (1 cup)

8 pitas, plus salata or pickles, kaymak or sour cream, and ajvar or roasted red peppers, for serving

In a large bowl, combine the beef and lamb and mix by hand. Add the minced onion, paprika, garlic powder, salt, and pepper and mix thoroughly with a wooden spoon. In a medium bowl, combine the cheeses.

Divide the meat into 16 balls, then form each ball into 5-inch round patties no more than ¼ inch thick. Lay 8 of the patties on a cutting board and place a heaping tablespoon of the cheese mix in the center of each patty.

Top with the remaining 8 patties and pinch the edges together to seal the cheese fully inside the meat. Gently form the meat into a proper hamburger shape without overworking.

Cook the burgers on a grill or in a hot cast-iron pan over medium-high heat, 10 to 12 minutes per side, until the meat is firm and melted cheese oozes out when you poke a hole in the burger. This is a well-done burger, cooked all the way through so that the cheese in the center melts. Let rest for 2 to 3 minutes and serve in the pitas with plenty of fixins'.

Makes 8 sloppy burgers

Francesinha

HOT CHEESE HANGOVER CURE

RECOMMENDED: *provolone*
SUBSTITUTIONS: *Havarti, fontina*

A Francesinha ("little Frenchie") is a Portuguese "inside-out" grilled cheese that's a cross between a croque madame and a French dip, with layers of savory meat sandwiched between bread draped in melted cheese and smothered in spiced gravy. Some versions are topped with a runny egg, and I say why not? Ham and linguiça (a smoked, cured Portuguese pork sausage) are traditional fillings, alongside roast beef. You can use leftover steak, if you have it, and cube steak or hamburger patties will do, too. I'd even put a Steak-umm® on this, because I'm not ashamed. Needless to say, this gut buster goes best after a night of drinking or as part of a seriously boozy brunch.

FOR THE LAZY GRAVY:

3 tablespoons butter

1 small shallot, diced (¼ cup)

1 garlic clove, peeled

1 bay leaf

2 sprigs fresh thyme
(or ½ teaspoon dried)

3 tablespoons all-purpose flour

¾ teaspoon kosher salt

½ teaspoon ground cumin

¼ teaspoon crushed red pepper flakes

¼ teaspoon freshly ground black pepper

⅓ cup dry red wine

¾ cup beef stock (homemade is best,
or low-sodium store-bought)

¾ cup chicken stock (ditto)

1 tablespoon Worcestershire sauce

1 tablespoon ketchup

FOR THE SANDWICHES:

2 small steaks, about 5 ounces each
(strip or cube steak are both good
choices)

1 tablespoon unsalted butter,
plus more for buttering bread

2 eggs

4 thick slices white bread

6 thin slices of ham, about 12 ounces

1 linguiça sausage, about 8 ounces,
cut into ½-inch-thick slices

8 (1-ounce) slices provolone

(continued)

MAKE THE GRAVY: In a medium saucepan over medium heat, melt 2 tablespoons of the butter until foaming. Add the shallot, garlic, bay leaf, and thyme and cook until the shallots soften, about 2 minutes. Whisk in the flour and continue to cook, stirring, for 1 more minute. Add the salt, cumin, red pepper flakes, and black pepper and cook for 1 more minute.

Slowly whisk in the wine, stocks, Worcestershire, and ketchup and continue to cook, stirring occasionally, until the gravy thickens, about 10 minutes. Discard the garlic clove, bay leaf, and thyme sprigs.

Take the gravy off the heat, whisk in the remaining tablespoon butter, and adjust the seasoning if needed. Cover the pan and set aside. (The gravy can be made ahead and reheated as needed. It will keep in the refrigerator for 1 week.)

MAKE THE SANDWICH: In a cast-iron pan, cook the steak to your liking and set aside. In the same pan, melt the butter and cook the eggs sunny-side up just until the whites set. Keep the yolks very runny, as they will continue to cook when you broil the sandwiches.

Preheat the broiler. Reheat the gravy over low heat.

Toast the bread in a toaster, then butter all 4 slices on one side. Place 2 pieces of toast, butter side up, in a glass baking dish with sides at least 1 or 2 inches high. Layer the toast with the steak, ham, and sausage, then top with the remaining toast, butter side down. Top each sandwich with a fried egg, then drape each with 4 slices of the cheese. Transfer to the oven and broil until the cheese is melted, about 5 minutes. Place the sandwiches on plates and ladle the hot gravy over and around them. Serve immediately.

Makes 1½ cups gravy and 2 sandwiches, antacid on the side

Thanksgiving Francesinha

My favorite part of Thanksgiving isn't the main meal—it's the sandwiches made from leftovers. (They're also the reason I don't overeat at the feast—gotta save room for sammies!) Layer roasted turkey, sliced ham (if you've got it), and any fresh or cured sausage. Have some sweet Italian sausage leftover from making stuffing? Grill it up! Some salami leftover from the big day's cheese board? That'll do! In truth, turkey with whatever meats are lying around will fill your Francesinha just fine. Now here comes the important part: draping the sandwich in plenty of cheese. Cheddar and/or Gruyère are my picks for turkey, since they melt well and give oomph where turkey falls flat (provolone is too mild for turkey). Whatever you choose, make sure the cheese gets good and melty, and don't forget to soak it all in gravy.

GRILLED CHEESE INSPIRATIONS
for When You're Feeling Extra

A classic grilled cheese is great, but sometimes you want to get down and dirty with a little something extra. These cheesy combinations answer the call:

EASY BRIE-ZY

Marin French Brie with Ursini Pestato di Funghi Porcini (porcini mushroom pesto) and Downey's Honey Butter

Sweet and earthy, like your favorite yoga instructor.

AMERICAN PLOUGHMAN'S

Beehive Cheese Co. Beehive Fresh plus Brooklyn Brine Co. Maple Bourbon Bread & Butter Pickles and crispy fried onions

Classic, but extra.

BACON LOVERS' SUPREME

Marieke Gouda Bacon with Bacon's Heir Malabar Black Pepper Pork Clouds (pork rinds)

Don't knock it 'til you try it.

HEAT SEEKER

Cabot Hot Habanero Cheddar plus Rick's Picks Smokra (spicy pickled okra) and Creminelli Salami Piccante

Have a refreshing beverage on hand.

Khachipuri
JUST A BOATLOAD OF CHEESE

Think of a khachipuri as a raft that's taking on water, except that, here, the raft is a pastry and the water, bubbling hot cheese. It's an appropriately nautical image for the national dish of Georgia, which sits on the eastern edge of the Black Sea, sandwiched between Turkey and Russia. The traditional cheese for khachipuri is called sulguni, a pungent, brined, stretched-curd affair. To approximate its texture and flavors, a mélange of mozzarella, feta, and chèvre does nicely. The mozzarella ensures melt, the feta keeps things salty, and the chèvre adds a smooth, creamy tanginess. Because of the two rises, this dough recipe takes some time. If you're short on it, store-bought pizza dough and even puff pastry are shortcuts, but you'll be rewarded if you make your own: the pastry is pillowy tender and deliciously rich.

1 cup whole milk

3 cups all-purpose flour, plus more for dusting and rolling

2 (.25-ounce) packets active dry yeast (2¼ teaspoons)

2 tablespoons sugar

½ teaspoon kosher salt

10 tablespoons (1¼ sticks) unsalted butter, cut into tablespoons and softened, plus 2 tablespoons unsalted butter, melted

Olive oil

16 ounces whole milk mozzarella, shredded (about 3 cups)

4 ounces chèvre, crumbled (1 cup)

4 ounces feta, crumbled (1 cup)

8 ounces ricotta (2 cups)

1 tablespoon dried oregano

In a small saucepan set on low, heat the milk with ½ cup water just to lukewarm (you don't want bubbles; remove it from the heat just as it starts to steam).

Mix 3 cups of the flour with the yeast, sugar, and salt in the bowl of a stand mixer fitted with a dough hook. Scatter the softened butter into the bowl and mix at medium-high speed until the dough has pea-sized crumbles, 4 to 5 minutes.

(continued)

Add the lukewarm milk and knead the dough on medium speed, stopping once or twice to scrape down the flour on the side of the bowl, until the dough is smooth, elastic, and just hinting at a bit of shine, about 7 minutes.

Place the dough in a large bowl brushed with olive oil, cover with plastic wrap, and let sit in the warmest spot in your kitchen until nearly doubled in volume, about 1 hour. Uncover the dough, gently punch it down, then return it to the bowl, re-cover with the plastic wrap, and let it sit for another 30 minutes.

Combine the mozzarella, chèvre, feta, ricotta, and oregano in a large bowl. Line 2 baking sheets with parchment paper.

Turn the dough onto a floured surface and divide it into 4 equal pieces. Shape each piece into a ball, then roll out each into a 9-inch circle with a rolling pin, lightly flouring the dough, rolling pin, and surface as needed to keep the dough from sticking. Place 2 rounds on each prepared baking sheet. Sprinkle one-quarter of the cheese onto each round, keeping a 1-inch border all the way around.

Roll up the edge nearest you about one-third of the way to the center, then roll the edge opposite you down by one-third to create two rolled edges. Pinch the ends together to create a shape like a boat or an eye, with a rolled edge all around and two sealed, pointed ends. Repeat with the remaining cheese and rounds. Once finished, cover each baking sheet with a clean dish towel and let the khachipuri rest and rise for 1 more hour. Preheat the oven to 375°F.

Brush the edges of the dough with the melted butter. Transfer the khachipuri to the oven and bake until the crust is lightly golden and the cheese is bubbling and browned, about 45 to 50 minutes. Once out of the oven, the cheese will be molten, so let them rest about 5 minutes before serving.

Makes 4 khachipuri to drown yourself in cheese

Red Wines for Khachipuri

Georgia has one of the oldest winemaking traditions in the world, dating back nearly eight thousand years. Both red and white wines are made there, primarily by small producers using traditional methods. Today it's possible to find Georgian wines at shops in the United States, but I won't send you on a hunt for something elusive (though if you're interested, they're worth seeking out). Instead, here are recommendations for medium-bodied, herbaceous red wines that are perfect pairings with oregano-flecked khachipuri.

KUNIN WINES SANTA BARBARA COUNTY SYRAH

Kunin Wines Santa Barbara County Syrah is a fruit-driven, youthful, easy-drinking California wine made entirely of Syrah. Its bright acidity plays nicely against the salty richness of the khachipuri cheese blend.

BERNARD BAUDRY CHINON LES GRANGES

Hailing from France's Loire Valley is Bernard Baudry Chinon Les Granges, an approachable, concentrated wine from Cabernet Franc, with vivid notes of cherry and raspberry.

VILLA RUSSIZ MERLOT COLLIO

Villa Russiz Merlot Collio is a jammy, decadent Italian merlot with whispering notes of cacao that's still somehow mellow enough to give the khachipuri room to shine.

CASA LAPOSTOLLE CARMENÈRE CUVÉE ALEXANDRE

Notes of blackberry jam and clove linger in Casa Lapostolle Carmenère Cuvée Alexandre, a medium- to full-bodied Chilean red made from Carmenère grapes.

'Sup, Soup?

UNTIL IT'S SOCIALLY ACCEPTABLE TO GUZZLE FONDUE STRAIGHT from the pot—live your best life!—you can best indulge your urge to shotgun liquefied cheese by slurping on cheesy soups. Luckily, that's no punishment. Soups warm us from the inside out, with stick-to-your-ribs nourishment during colder months.

The staying power of cheesy soups lies in their calories, those much-maligned units of heat measurement that are really just a metric, like meters or miles. More often than not, we view calories as enemy number one, but food is fuel, and calories are how we measure the fuel content of our food. Fats have the highest concentration of calories at nine per gram (pure alcohol clocks in second, at seven per gram).

As a high-fat food, cheese is literally superfuel, a long-burning source of energy perfect for powering us through intense physical activity and cold weather. And it tastes amazing, whether an emulsification of hot cheddar, as in Broccoli Cheddar Soup (see page 111), or a flotilla of blue in a brothy stew, as in Colcannon Stew with Bacon & Blue Cheese (see page 108).

You can double down on your cheesy soups by adding Parmesan rinds to homemade stocks and soups. Once you've grated what you can from them, store them in the freezer and add them to stocks and soups during the simmering stage. They bring an extra layer of flavor and act as a subtle but impactful thickener. And don't be afraid to add them to all types of soup for a little je ne sais quoi, whether cheese-laden or not. Just remember to fish them out before you sup.

French Onion Soup

EVERYONE LOVES A BREAD BOWL

TRADITIONAL: *Gruyère*

What's not to love about a giant loaf of bread brimming with caramelized onions, swimming in beef broth, and draped in melted cheese? Nothing. But be warned: this is a messy communal soup, meant to be slurped and eventually deconstructed with friends. Gruyère is the go-to here. If you must, other alpine cheeses would suffice, but adhering to tradition pays off: Gruyère yodels back at the bread, beef broth, and onions—a flavor echo if there ever was one. Channel patience when caramelizing the onions, which takes more time than you'd expect: forty-five minutes to an hour. Read a book. Eat a peanut butter and jelly sandwich. Fold some laundry. It's worth it to resist the urge to rush.

1 large boule of hearty bread
(übercrusty and dark is best)

2 tablespoons olive oil

2 pounds Vidalia or Spanish onions
(about 4), halved and thinly sliced

4 tablespoons (½ stick) unsalted butter

1 bay leaf

4 sprigs fresh thyme

1 teaspoon kosher salt

½ teaspoon freshly ground black pepper

1 tablespoon Worcestershire sauce

1 cup dry white wine

5 cups beef stock (homemade is best,
or low-sodium store-bought)

12 (¼-inch-thick) slices Gruyère

Preheat the oven to 350°F. Cut off the top of the boule and scoop out as much of the bread as possible (be careful not to puncture the crust). Reserve the bread and the top for a later use (freeze them in a plastic bag for the next time you need breadcrumbs). Place the hollowed-out bread on a large baking sheet and toast in the oven for 15 minutes.

In a large heavy-bottomed soup pot over medium heat, warm the olive oil until fragrant and shimmering. Add the onions and cook, stirring occasionally, until they begin to sweat, about 10 minutes.

(continued)

Add the butter, bay leaf, thyme, salt, and pepper and stir to combine. Reduce the heat to medium-low and cook, stirring occasionally, until the onions are a deep golden color, 45 minutes to 1 hour.

Add the Worcestershire and wine and simmer until the liquid is evaporated, about 10 minutes. Add the beef stock and continue to simmer for another 30 minutes to bring the flavors of the soup together.

Preheat the broiler. Take the soup off the heat and remove the bay leaf and thyme sprigs. Carefully pour the hot soup into the toasted bread shell, and drape the soup and boule with the sliced Gruyère. Carefully transfer the baking sheet to the oven and broil until the cheese melts, bubbles, and browns, 7 to 8 minutes. Serve immediately, with big spoons and plenty of napkins.

Serves 4 to 6 lucky loafers

STOCK TIPS
A Simple Guide to Making Stock

Soup is 100 percent better when made with homemade stock, but for some folks the prospect of preparing stock is daunting. There are plenty of basic recipes for vegetable, seafood, and meat stocks all over the Internet, so here are some supplemental stock tips to get you closer to a liquid gold mine:

HOLY TRINITY

Onions, carrots, and celery are the building blocks of every stock. I usually go for a 1:1:1 ratio of one onion, one carrot, and one celery stalk.

ROAST

Roasting any of the meat or vegetable components of your stock will concentrate the flavors and make a deeply flavored stock.

COLD WATER (& WINE!)

Certain proteins will only dissolve in cold water, so start your stock with cold water. A little acidity is also an important tool in breaking down ingredients and extracting their flavor, so add some wine *(a 6:1 ratio of water to wine)*.

HERB INDEX

Bay leaf, fresh thyme, some parsley—fresh herbs enhance stock. Add them at the beginning of the stock-making process, so they have plenty of time to impart their subtle flavors during cooking.

SALT WITH CARE

The whole point of stock is to extract and concentrate flavors as water simmers and evaporates. Remember that any salt you add in the early stages will concentrate as water evaporates. Err on the side of less salt, always. (Some cooks don't salt their stock at all, preferring to adjust seasoning when they employ the stock in whatever they're cooking.)

Colcannon Stew with Bacon & Blue Cheese

PURPLE REIGN

RECOMMENDED: *Cashel Blue*

SUBSTITUTIONS: *Rogue Creamery Caveman Blue, Old Chatham Sheepherding Ewe's Blue*

Briny blue cheese and smoky bacon are the backbone of this riff on colcannon, a traditional Irish dish made with cabbage, mashed potatoes, and copious amounts of dairy (always butter, sometimes cheese). In this stew-y version, purple cabbage is a cruciferous canvas for the seaweedy flavors of Ireland's most famous blue cheese, Cashel Blue. A zesty slaw finishes the stew with a zinger of a last word, in the great Irish tradition.

5 tablespoons unsalted butter

3 slices thick-cut bacon (about 4 ounces), diced

1 medium yellow onion, diced (1 cup)

12 cups shredded purple cabbage (about ½ medium head)

1 cup dry white wine

1 pound Peruvian purple or Yukon Gold potatoes (about 2 medium), peeled and cut in ½-inch dice

1 tablespoon kosher salt

2 cups chicken or vegetable stock (homemade is best, or low-sodium store-bought)

½ cup roughly chopped flat-leaf parsley

3 tablespoons extra virgin olive oil

2 tablespoons red wine vinegar

Freshly ground black pepper

½ cup heavy cream

8 ounces blue cheese, crumbled (about ½ cup)

In a large heavy-bottomed soup pot over medium heat, melt 1 tablespoon of the butter, then add the bacon and onion and sauté until the bacon is rendered and the onions begin to caramelize around the edges, about 15 minutes.

Melt 2 more tablespoons of butter into the bacon-onion mixture, then add 9 cups of cabbage to the pot, stir to combine the ingredients, and sauté until the cabbage is shiny and just beginning to wilt, about 10 minutes.

(continued)

Add the wine, potatoes, and salt and cook until half of the wine evaporates, about 10 minutes. Add the stock, increase the heat to high, and bring to a boil. Cover the pot and reduce the heat to low. Simmer until the potatoes are tender, about 20 minutes.

While the soup simmers, toss the remaining shredded cabbage with the parsley in a mixing bowl. Dress with the olive oil and red wine vinegar, season to taste with salt and pepper, and stir to combine.

When the potatoes are easily pierced by a paring knife, uncover the pot and stir the remaining 2 tablespoons butter into the stew, then stir in the cream and simmer uncovered for 5 minutes. Reserve one-quarter of the blue cheese crumbles, then melt the remainder into the stew. Ladle the stew into bowls, then top with a bit of the slaw and the reserved blue cheese. Serve immediately.

Serves 4 to cure the winter blues

FLAVOR & FAT
The Lowdown on Cooking with Blue Cheese

Think of blue cheese as you would butter or cream—something to meld into a dish, rather than something to melt on its own. Flavor and fat is this category's main attraction; don't count on blues for a stretchy melt, they won't deliver. Instead, focus on flavor: blue cheeses run the gamut from soft, relatively mild, lightly marbled blues, like Gorgonzola Cremificato, to full-bodied, craggy blues, like Roquefort (generally, the more visually present the blue mold, the more intensely flavored the cheese). Consider how forceful you want to go (this is largely dependent on what the other elements of the dish are), then think about texture. Creamier blues will melt into smooth pools of umami-laced cream; drier, more mottled blues will give a melt that finishes with more grit.

Broccoli Cheddar Soup

DINER FOR DINNER

TRUSTED BRANDS: *Cabot Creamery, Grafton Village Cheese Cheddar*

From the can, or by the cup at your local diner, broccoli cheddar soup is pure comfort food. Chunky or smooth, it benefits from a garnish of Wisconsin Caviar (aka fried cheese curds). Come for the broccoli, but stay for the butter, cream, and cheese.

4 tablespoons (½ stick) unsalted butter

1 small yellow onion, diced

1 medium carrot, diced

1 celery stalk, diced

2 garlic cloves, minced

1 bay leaf

1½ teaspoons kosher salt

¼ teaspoon freshly ground black pepper

2 tablespoons all-purpose flour

1 cup heavy cream

3 cups chicken or vegetable stock (homemade is best, or low-sodium store-bought)

1 large head broccoli, broken into small florets and stems chopped (about 4 cups), or 4 cups frozen broccoli, thawed

8 ounces cheddar, shredded (about 2 cups)

2 tablespoons grated Parmigiano Reggiano

1 pound Wisconsin Caviar (see page 70), for garnish (optional)

In a large heavy-bottomed soup pot, melt the butter over medium heat. Add the onion and cook until translucent, 6 to 7 minutes. Add the carrot, celery, garlic, bay leaf, salt, and pepper and give it a stir. Cook until the garlic is fragrant and just beginning to color, about 5 minutes.

Add the flour and mix to coat the vegetables. Cook, stirring, until the mixture is golden and smells nutty, about 4 minutes. Stir in the heavy cream and bring to a simmer. Cook for 2 minutes to thicken the mixture. Whisk in the stock, add the broccoli, and simmer uncovered until the broccoli is fork tender, about 20 minutes.

(continued)

Remove from the heat, discard the bay leaf, and puree in a blender or with an immersion blender (I like a relatively smooth soup, with a few small chunks of broccoli, but you can go supersmooth or chunky, according to preference). If using a blender, return the soup to the pot and set over medium heat. If using an immersion blender, set the pot over the heat. Once the soup returns to a simmer, whisk in the shredded cheddar and grated Parmigiano Reggiano in four batches, adding the next batch only after the previous has melted. Adjust the seasoning if needed, and serve. If you're garnishing with fried cheese curds, keep the soup warm while frying the curds, then drop some hot fried curds into the soup before serving.

Serves 4 for cruciferous curd-slurping

Potato, Cheese, & Corn Soup

SOPA LOCRO DE PAPA

RECOMMENDED: *Tillamook Monterey Jack, Mozzarella Company Queso Fresco*

Sopa locro de papa is a double dose of hot cheese, with Monterey Jack and queso fresco melded into a smoky potato and corn base. It's ubiquitous throughout the Andean region, one that every abuela customizes. This sopa is all about the fixings: traditional favorites that'll make you feel frisky include fresh cilantro, avocado, hot sauce for heat, and cancha (corn nuts) for crunch.

2 tablespoons olive oil

1 tablespoon unsalted butter

1 small yellow onion, diced (½ cup)

2 garlic cloves, minced

1 teaspoon ground cumin

1 teaspoon annatto powder

1 bay leaf

1 teaspoon kosher salt

2 pounds russet potatoes (about 3 large), peeled and cut into ½-inch cubes

4 cups chicken or vegetable stock (homemade is best, or low-sodium store-bought)

1 cup heavy cream

1 cup fresh corn kernels (from about 1 to 2 ears), or frozen in a pinch

4 ounces Monterey Jack, shredded (1 cup)

4 ounces queso fresco, crumbled (1 cup), plus more for garnish

Freshly ground black pepper

Chopped cilantro, sliced avocado, corn nuts, and hot sauce, for garnish

Preheat the oven to 350°F.

In a large heavy-bottomed soup pot over medium heat, warm the olive oil and butter until the butter foams. Cook the onion until soft, stirring occasionally, about 5 minutes. Add the garlic, cumin, annatto, bay leaf, and salt and cook until the onions are translucent, another 5 minutes. Add the potatoes, stir to coat in the onion mixture, and cook 1 more minute.

(continued)

Pour in the stock, increase the heat to medium-high, and bring to a boil. Cover the pot, reduce the heat to low, and simmer until the potatoes are fork tender, about 20 minutes.

With a potato masher or wooden spoon, gently smash the potatoes into pea-sized pieces. Stir in the cream and add the corn. Increase the heat to medium and bring the soup back up to a simmer, about 5 minutes.

Whisk in the Monterey Jack a handful at a time, adding more cheese only after the previous handful has melted, then stir in the queso fresco and cook for another 5 minutes. Adjust the seasoning with salt and pepper if needed, transfer the soup to single-serving bowls, and garnish with the cilantro, avocado, corn nuts, hot sauce, and queso fresco.

Serves 6 for a main course

Fresh Cheeses for Filling & Finishing

Fresh cheeses are the most direct pathway to the tiny miracle that is cheese—and they are the simplest cheeses to make (until the early to mid-twentieth century, most fresh cheeses were made in the home or on a very small scale). They're excellent for fillings (see Cheese Manicotti 4G, page 140) and for adding a last-minute flourish of fat (remember, fat is flavor) to casseroles, soups, and salads.

FARMER CHEESE

Farmer cheese sits squarely in the homemade cheese tradition, and shares a geneology with cottage cheese. Modern commercial versions of farmer cheese are mild, and crumble into small curds. They're a good choice for topping dishes that require fat and texture, like full-bodied soups or meats, rather than dishes needing a complex flavor infusion.

COTTAGE CHEESE

Cottage cheese is a good binding cheese, best used in concert with a starch, as its high-moisture content makes it very loose (see Kugel with Cottage Cheese, Leeks, & Dill, page 148). The little pearls of creamy curd are its defining, charming feature.

RICOTTA

Everyone loves ricotta, and that's because it's versatile, delicious, and as creamy as a fresh curd cheese can be. It's best used to top recipes headed for the oven, such as gratins or baked pastas. Because of its high-moisture content, it's a little too wet for topping salads or soups.

CHÈVRE

Chèvre turns out quite a bit of flavor for a fresh cheese, namely a bright acidity backed up by notes of lemon and fresh grass. It's by far one of the densest fresh cheeses, so if you're using it as a filling, you will likely need to cut it with a looser, wetter cheese (like ricotta). Because of its density, it's equally applicable as a raw topping crumbled over salads and soups, or baked into and onto casseroles.

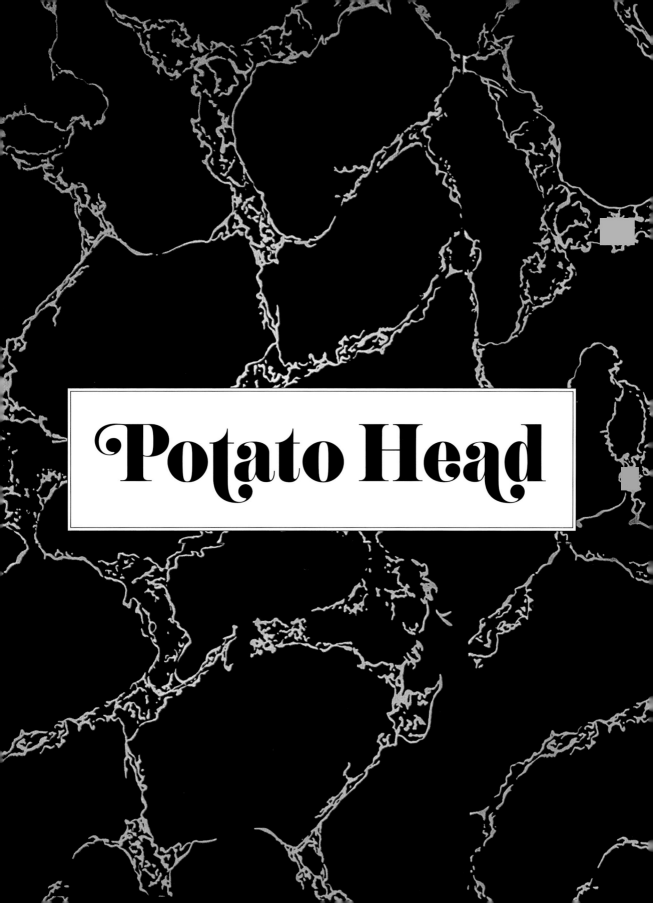

Potato Head

OTATOES PUT OUT FOR BUTTERFAT; WITHOUT IT, THEY literally leave us mealymouthed. And while butter is good, and sour cream is cool, nothing dresses up a potato like cheese, turning timid tubers into luscious, lip-smacking spuds.

Of course, all fats add a flair that potatoes so desperately need, but cheese lends something special: unbeatable textural variation. Like potatoes, cheese shape-shifts depending on how you cook it. With slow, controlled heat, it's all smooth moves; with high heat, it's crispy for days. Combined, they amplify each other.

There's something especially thrilling about taking an inexpensive, everyday food like a potato—something that's pretty bland all by its lonesome—and pairing it with something as complex, decadent, and crave-worthy as cheese. It's an easy elevation that showcases the best of both ingredients. And there's nothing wrong with easy. Some things shouldn't be hard.

In the United States, cheesy potatoes are typically served as a side dish, but in Europe they're often center table. Cheese makes it possible, adding the protein and fat that take potatoes from side dish to main attraction. A lightly dressed salad of seasonal greens is all the backup a cheesy potato needs to be ready for prime time.

Aligot

TUBER FONDUE

TRADITIONAL: *Cantal, Laguiole, Tomme d'Auvergne*
SUBSTITUTIONS: *Spring Brook Farm Reading, Grafton Village Truffle Cheddar*

Aligot is what happens when a copious amount of cheese melts into mashed potatoes, creating a luscious fondue-mash hybrid. This recipe doesn't strictly adhere to tradition—no one from France would ever make aligot with mozzarella—*jamais!*—but sometimes it's the destination not the journey, right? Mozzarella adds a stable, easy melt that's insurance for whatever cheese you choose to use, guaranteeing the elastic pull that's aligot's decadent calling card.

2 pounds Yukon Gold potatoes (about 4 medium), peeled and cut into 1-inch cubes

1 tablespoon kosher salt

¾ cup heavy cream

1 garlic clove, grated on a zester

8 ounces (2 sticks) unsalted butter, softened

½ teaspoon white pepper

12 ounces cheese of choice, shredded (3 cups)

8 ounces mozzarella, shredded (2 cups)

Place the potatoes and salt in a medium saucepan and cover with cool water. Cover the pan with a lid and bring to a boil over high heat. Reduce the heat and simmer until the potatoes are fork-tender, about 15 minutes. In a small saucepan, warm the cream over low heat.

Drain the potatoes and return them to the saucepan over low heat. Mash them with a potato masher until they are very smooth with minimal lumps. (Lumps are groove killers. Take your time here and really have at them.) Stir in the grated garlic.

Stir in the butter 1 tablespoon at a time, incorporating completely before the next addition. Once all of the butter is melted into the potatoes, add the warm cream in two batches, stirring continuously until smooth and creamy. Stir in the white pepper. If you have an immersion blender, use that to tackle any remaining lumps. If you don't, give the potatoes one last go with the masher.

Add the shredded cheeses a handful at a time, stirring vigorously until the potatoes and cheese have combined into a smooth elasticity that resembles pizza dough. Adjust the seasoning if needed. Serve immediately in big bowls with a spoon, or forgo the utensils and use pieces of bread to shovel the aligot into your face, like old French men do.

Makes enough starchy fondue for 4

Potato Gratin with Pancetta & Leeks

FUNKY SPUDS

RECOMMENDED: *Taleggio, Meadow Creek Dairy Grayson, Quadrello di Bufala*

I prefer using supple, slightly funky washed-rind cheeses in gratins. Since they shouldn't actually use that much cheese, I figure a whiffy one won't threaten the harmony of the dish. Cream does quite a bit of the heavy lifting in this gratin. If the cream is the garment, pungent cheese is the statement necklace that really makes the outfit. But gratins can also be a great way to use up a hodgepodge of leftover cheese, so don't get too caught up in my mixed metaphors: use what you have, a good melter for inside and something aged (see Finishing Cheeses, page 125) that'll crisp up nicely on top.

6 tablespoons unsalted butter, plus more for greasing the pan

4 ounces pancetta, finely diced

2 leeks, white and light green parts only, washed and thinly sliced

2 sprigs fresh thyme

2 garlic cloves, minced

1 teaspoon kosher salt

1 pound russet potatoes (about 2 medium), peeled and sliced $\frac{1}{8}$ inch thick

1 pound Yukon Gold potatoes (about 2 medium), peeled and sliced $\frac{1}{8}$ inch thick

Freshly ground black pepper

6 ounces Taleggio, cubed

1½ cups heavy cream

2 tablespoons grated Parmigiano Reggiano

Preheat the oven to 375°F. Butter a 9 x 13-inch glass baking dish.

In a medium sauté pan over medium heat, melt 1 tablespoon of the butter. Add the pancetta and cook until crisp, about 5 minutes. Remove with a slotted spoon to a small bowl and set aside. In the rendered fat, sauté the leeks and the thyme until the leeks are soft and bright green, about 5 minutes. Add the garlic and salt and sauté until fragrant, about 2 minutes. Remove the pan from the heat and discard the thyme.

(continued)

Cut the remaining 5 tablespoons butter into ½-inch cubes. Shingle the potatoes in a single layer on the bottom of the baking dish, alternating slices of each type, then add a few gridings of black pepper. Scatter about 2 tablespoons of the leek mixture onto the potatoes, then sprinkle on some pancetta, 5 or 6 cubes of Taleggio, and 4 or 5 cubes of butter. Repeat, layering the sliced potatoes, leek mixture, pancetta, Taleggio, and butter, and seasoning with freshly ground black pepper every other layer. Finish with a potato layer and press the layers down into the dish (you should have about 5 layers). Pour the cream over the potatoes, dot with the remaining butter, and sprinkle with the Parmigiano Reggiano.

Transfer the baking dish to the oven and bake until bubbling, browned, and crispy on top, about 60 minutes. Let cool for 20 minutes before serving—the gratin definitely "comes together" during this time—and so you don't burn your mouth, either.

Serves 6 to 10, depending on when served during the meal

FINISHING CHEESES

Like Salt, Like Breadcrumbs, but Cheese

As cheese ages, it loses moisture to the environment, concentrating its flavor and making it more resistant to melt (see **Sizzlers**, page 30). Because of this, drier, aged cheeses—such as Parmesan, Gouda, and Manchego—are often applied as "finishing cheeses" on pastas or salads or grated onto casseroles headed for the oven. These cheeses are an umami-laden, saltlike seasoning that can also act as a crust when baked. They also work as a thickener, binding dressings, sauces, and soups.

Chorizo, Egg, & Cheese Baked Potato

GET LOADED

There was a brief moment in time when my aerobics-loving, wheat germ–worshipping mother—who almost never allowed me the salty nectar of fast food—would take me to the Wendy's Baked Potato Bar. She must've assumed we could squeeze a healthy meal out of the convenience, but she was misguided: cheese and bacon were the preferred paint for my baked potato canvas. Nary a piece of broccoli sullied my baked potato. But I truly perfected my own private Idaho later in life, when I swapped salty-smoky bacon for smoky-spicy chorizo, put an egg on top, and smothered the whole thing in mascarpone—a testament to childhood rebellion enduring well into middle age.

4 large russet potatoes

1 tablespoon olive oil

1½ cups Mornay Sauce (see page 18)

2 fresh chorizos, casings discarded (about 8 ounces sausage)

2 tablespoons white vinegar

4 eggs

4 tablespoons (½ stick) unsalted butter

Kosher salt and freshly ground black pepper

4 ounces mascarpone, at room temperature

4 tablespoons minced chives

Preheat the oven to 350°F.

Rinse the potatoes well and puncture them all over several times with a fork. Rub them with the olive oil, place them on a baking rack set on a baking sheet and bake for 75 minutes, until a fork easily glides into the center of the potato.

While the potatoes are cooking, make a half batch of the Mornay Sauce. Once the sauce is finished, cover the pan with a lid to keep the sauce warm.

(continued)

Place a cast-iron or sauté pan over medium heat and crumble in the chorizo. Cook the chorizo until browned, about 7 to 9 minutes then drain on paper towels and set aside.

When the baked potatoes are ready, remove them from the oven and let them cool slightly while you poach the eggs. In a medium saucepan, bring 3 cups water just to a boil, then pour into a medium heatproof bowl and set aside. In the same saucepan, bring another 3 cups water and the vinegar to a simmer—don't let it reach a full boil. Crack 1 egg into a small bowl or demitasse cup. With the handle of a wooden spoon, vigorously swirl the water in the saucepan to create a whirlpool. Slowly slide the egg into the water and poach until the whites are firm, about 3 minutes. Gently remove it from the simmering water with a spider into the reserved bowl of hot water. Repeat with the remaining eggs.

Cut each potato end to end to a depth of 1 inch, then push the ends toward each other, creating a pocket at the top of the potato. Drop a tablespoon of butter into each pocket. Season with salt and freshly ground black pepper. Top each potato with one-quarter of the Mornay sauce, some of the crumbled chorizo, one-quarter of the mascarpone, a poached egg, and chives. Serve immediately.

Serves 4 for spud worship

Welcome to the Melt, Stretch, & Sizzle Baked Potato Bar, How May I Help You?

Build a baked potato bar using the sauces in Saucy (see page 16), a few simply cooked ingredients, and some purchased condiments.

MORNAY, PART DEUX

A perfectly baked potato plus Mornay Sauce, with roasted brussels sprouts and Quince & Apple Shallot Confit with Red Wine

FONDUTA

A perfectly baked potato plus Truffle Fonduta, with roasted mushrooms, and crushed Torres Black Truffle Potato Chips

RAREBIT, PART DEUX

A perfectly baked potato plus Rarebit Sauce, with grilled steak tips, caramelized onions, and Preservation & Co. Hefeweizen Bread & Butter Sweet Cucumber Chips

BLUE CHEESE

A perfectly baked potato plus Blue Cheese Sauce, with pulled or shredded cooked chicken and Olympia Provisions Pickled Celery

Poutine
with Lazy Gravy
CANADIAN CURD

TRUSTED BRANDS: *See Cheddar, Interrupted, page 81*

French fries and cheese curds bathed in gravy are Quebec's venerable contribution to the hot cheese canon. Poutine is an almost poetic juxtaposition of crispy, melty, and saucy, taken just to the edge of too salty. In other words, it's perfect drinking food, and especially compatible with a rich amber or dark beer. For the ultimate combination of textures, room temperature cheese curds, hot fries, and bubbling hot gravy are all a must here, so the curds get perfectly soft and melty.

2 pounds russet potatoes (about 4 medium), cut into ¼-inch matchsticks

1½ cups Lazy Gravy (see page 94), hot

Frying oil (see A Quick Guide to Frying Oils, page 80)

Kosher salt

1 pound cheese curds

¼ cup finely chopped flat-leaf parsley

Put the matchstick potatoes in a large bowl and cover with cold water. Soak for 30 minutes, then drain them and soak them again in another batch of fresh, cold water for another 30 minutes. Drain and dry thoroughly on paper towels. While the potatoes soak, make the Lazy Gravy; if necessary, reheat the gravy before serving.

Pour the oil into a deep heavy-bottomed pan to a depth of 5 inches. Heat on medium to 350°F. Fry the potatoes in two batches, stirring and turning them with a spider, until they separate, float to the surface, and they're very lightly golden and show signs of shrinkage, about 5 minutes. Transfer them to a baking sheet lined with brown paper or paper towels to drain.

Once all the potatoes are fried, increase the heat of the oil to 425°F and fry the potatoes again, in two batches, until crisp and deep golden, another 5 minutes.

Drain them again on the same baking sheet lined with fresh brown paper or paper towels. Generously salt the hot fries and place them on a serving platter. Scatter the cheese curds over the fries and pour the gravy over everything. Garnish with parsley and serve immediately.

Serves 2 to 4, dependent on parameters of propriety

Frico

LOVE, ITALIAN STYLE

TRADITONAL: *Asiago, Montasio, Piave*
SUBSTITUTION: *young Manchego*

Frico is a savory potato and cheese skillet cake from Friuli that's similar to the French tartiflette or the Spanish tortilla. It's typically made with semi-hard, high-fat cheeses from Veneto. A good frico is all about the crisp and the flip, so set yourself up for success with a medium-moisture cheese and a well-seasoned cast-iron pan (if you feel unsteady using cast-iron, then a quality nonstick skillet is fine). I happen to like a bit of skin, so usually peel only half the potatoes and leave the rest skin-on, but you do you.

1 pound Yukon Gold potatoes (about 3 medium), cut into 1-inch cubes

1 tablespoon kosher salt

4 tablespoons olive oil

1 small yellow onion, finely chopped (¼ cup)

2 garlic cloves, minced

4 ounces cheese of choice, shredded (1 cup)

Freshly ground black pepper

2 tablespoons finely chopped flat-leaf parsley

Good extra virgin olive oil or chili-infused oil, for finishing

Place the cubed potatoes in a medium saucepan and cover with cool water. Add the salt and cover the pan. Bring the potatoes to a boil over high heat, then reduce the heat to medium-low and simmer until the potatoes are fork-tender, about 12 minutes. Drain the potatoes, then transfer them to a medium bowl, and smash them with a fork until they are broken up but still a bit chunky.

Heat 2 tablespoons of the olive oil in a medium cast-iron or nonstick pan over medium heat until fragrant. Add the onions and sauté until just browned at the edges, about 4 minutes. Add the garlic and cook until fragrant, 1 more minute or so. Transfer the onion and garlic to the bowl with the potatoes, then mix in the cheese and season with pepper.

(continued)

In the same pan used to cook the onions, heat the remaining 2 tablespoons olive oil over medium heat until almost smoking. Tilt the pan to coat it evenly with the oil, then add the potato mixture to the pan. Press the mixture down firmly and cook undisturbed until brown and crisp on the bottom, about 20 minutes.

Run a butter knife around the edges of the pan, slowly working it toward the center to help release it when you flip it over to cook the other side. Place a large plate over the top of the pan, and pressing down evenly on the plate, flip the pan. Return the pan to the heat and slide the frico back into it, browned side up, to cook the other side, another 10 minutes.

Turn onto a platter, sprinkle with parsley, drizzle with the best extra virgin olive oil you have—better still, some chili oil—and serve immediately.

Serves 2 for lunch or 4 for as an appetizer

Another Day, Another Frico

Frico is also the name for lacy Italian cheese crackers, made by baking grated low-moisture cheeses, such as Montasio, Grana Padano, or Parmigiano Reggiano, until crisp. (Aged Manchego or aged Gouda are also suitable options.)

Preheat the oven to 375°F.

Combine ½ cup grated low-moisture cheese with ¼ teaspoon freshly ground black pepper.

Mound tablespoons of the cheese 2 inches apart on a baking sheet lined with a silicone baking mat. Lightly press the mounds down into 2-inch circles. Bake about 5 minutes, until bubbly and browned.

Cool completely before serving. Best served with a crisp glass of white wine from the same region as the cheese.

Pasta Lovers

CODEPENDENT RELATIONSHIPS USUALLY GET A BAD RAP, AND truth be told they're not the best look. But I fully support the hot-mess coupling that is cheese and pasta. What was life like before they hooked up? Gosh, I don't know. It seems like they've been together forever.

Like many enmeshed romances, cheese and pasta cling to each other as if their lives depended on it. Pasta absorbs the flavors of cheese, and cheese melts willingly into pasta, combining in a succulent, sticky sum greater than its parts—a power couple for the ages.

I can't choose a favorite cheesy pasta. I love each in its own special way, tucking into any and every combination imaginable with genuine gusto. To choose one would be a betrayal of all the others, a twisted experiment in pasta Darwinism. And yet, I've made my choices here.

The recipes in this love letter to a dynamic duo represent something essential about the relationship between pasta and cheese, and admittedly also reflect my personal preferences. I couldn't not include a mac and cheese, though I did go for a rendition with plenty of drama (there's a whole burrata baked inside!). Stuffed pasta is represented by manicotti, here ricotta corseted in crêpes. The dish can be made with store-bought pasta shells, but homemade crêpes are far superior. This version stands up to any baked pasta dish (I'm looking at you, baked ziti). Käsespätzle makes an appearance because Germans know the love pairing that is noodles and cheese about as well as Italians, though in a less prodigious fashion. And I just adore kugel, the warm, grandmotherly hug that is egg noodles and cottage cheese, and the simplicity of the preparation.

Ultimately, all of the recipes capture the carb-y comfort of the genre. Cheese and pasta are deep into the sweatpants-and-chill phase of their relationship, and that's totally cool. Whenever they're together, it's all good.

Burrata Mac & Cheese

PEARL CREAM

CHEESE OF CHOICE: *cheddar, alpine, young Gouda*
RECOMMENDED: *BelGioioso burrata*

On the surface this is a classic béchamel-based mac, with the homey touch of diced ham and peas and a crown of crispy, chunky, parsley-flecked fresh breadcrumbs. But dig in and you'll find a whole burrata tucked inside—a creamy, silky, milky jewel just waiting to be plucked and pulled from a luscious bed of cheesy shells.

Kosher salt

3 cups Mornay Sauce (see page 18)

1 cup cubed baguette

2 tablespoons unsalted butter, melted

¼ cup finely chopped flat-leaf parsley

1 pound small pasta shells

1 cup frozen peas

1 cup diced ham

8 ounces cheese of choice, shredded (2 cups)

1 (4-ounce) burrata

Preheat the oven to 350°F. Boil a large pot of salted water.

Make the Mornay Sauce. Cover the pan with a lid to keep the sauce warm.

Pulse the baguette cubes in a food processor until the crumbs are pea-sized, about 5 pulses. Toss the breadcrumbs with the melted butter, then mix in the chopped parsley and set aside.

Cook the pasta according to the package instructions until just al dente. Drain well, then return the pasta to the pot and stir in the Mornay, peas, and ham. Stir three-quarters of the shredded cheese into the pasta, then pour half of the pasta into a 2-quart baking dish or casserole. Place the burrata in the center, then cover with the rest of the pasta. Top with the remaining shredded cheese, and then the breadcrumbs. Bake for 35 to 40 minutes, until bubbling, crisp, and browned.

Serves 6 to 8 cheese-loving guests

Cheese Manicotti 4G

CRÊPES AREN'T PASTA, BUT WHATEVER

TRUSTED BRAND: *BelGioiso*

My favorite manicotti are the ones my grandmother made, replacing pasta with fresh crêpes as soft and downy as the tissues she tucked in the sleeve of her housecoat. She served her manicotti in lieu of a pasta course, and we happily ate it as a comparable substitution. She filled the crêpes with airy, basil-flecked ricotta and then smothered them in a fresh, buttery tomato sauce. Needless to say, I ate as many as I could when she made them. I make my manicotti just as she did, in my great-grandmother's perfectly sized 6-inch cast-iron pan, passed down through the generations.

FOR THE FILLING:

16 ounces whole milk ricotta (2 cups)

1 egg, lightly beaten

10 basil leaves, finely chopped

¼ teaspoon kosher salt

Freshly ground black pepper

FOR THE SAUCE:

3 very large ripe tomatoes (2 pounds)

1 tablespoon olive oil

8 tablespoons (1 stick) unsalted butter

1 small onion, finely chopped (¼ cup)

4 garlic cloves, minced

1 teaspoon kosher salt

Freshly ground black pepper

FOR THE CRÊPES:

2 eggs

1 cup all-purpose flour

¼ teaspoon kosher salt

Olive oil, for greasing the crêpe pan

FOR THE ASSEMBLY:

½ cup grated Parmesan

(continued)

MAKE THE FILLING:

In a medium bowl, combine the ricotta, egg, basil, salt, and pepper to taste. Refrigerate the mixture until you're ready to assemble the manicotti.

MAKE THE SAUCE:

Slash the tomato skins with a knife before trimming and quartering them (this helps the skin break down during cooking).

In a large saucepan over medium heat, warm the olive oil and 1 tablespoon of the butter until bubbling, then add the onion and sauté, stirring occasionally, until translucent, about 7 minutes.

Add 4 more tablespoons of the butter, and once the butter melts, add the garlic and then the tomatoes, placing them deliberately in the pan, flesh-side down (the pan will be crowded). Crush the tomatoes lightly with a potato masher. Add the salt and pepper to taste, then cover and continue to cook the tomatoes until they release their juices, about 10 minutes.

Uncover the pot and mash the tomatoes with the potato masher until pulverized (it'll take some elbow grease, so put your arm into it). Re-cover and continue to cook for another 15 minutes.

Reduce the heat to low, uncover the pot, and crush the tomatoes one last time with the potato masher. Continue simmering the sauce over low heat, stirring occasionally, about 40 minutes, until the tomatoes have broken down into a thin sauce. Stir in the remaining butter and cook for another 5 minutes. Remove from the heat and use a pair of tongs to pick out some of the larger pieces of tomato skin, if you like. Don't fuss too much over this—skins in the sauce are okay. Adjust the seasoning if needed and set aside.

MAKE THE CRÊPES:

Line a baking sheet with parchment paper. Whisk the eggs and 1½ cups water in a medium bowl, then whisk in the flour and salt to make a thin batter.

Heat a small cast-iron or nonstick pan over medium-low heat until a drop of water sizzles and splatters, about 5 minutes. Once the pan is hot enough, lightly brush it with olive oil. Ladle ¼ cup of batter into the preheated pan and cook just until the edges curl and a colored ring appears around the perimeter, 1 to 2 minutes.

Run a wide, thin spatula around the edges to loosen the crêpe and flip it. Cook until the second side just starts to show some color, another 1 to 2 minutes, then remove the crêpe to the prepared baking sheet. Brush the pan with more olive oil and repeat until all the batter is used. You should have 16 crêpes.

ASSEMBLE AND BAKE THE MANICOTTI:

Preheat the oven to 350°F. Spread half the sauce onto the bottom of a 9 x 13-inch baking dish.

On a clean work surface, spoon 1 tablespoon of the ricotta filling onto the center of a crêpe. Roll the edge of the crêpe nearest you up toward the center over the filling, then roll the opposite edge of the crêpe downward, so that it forms a 1½-inch-wide tube.

Place each rolled crêpe, seam side down, in the baking dish. Repeat until the dish is full.

Pour the rest of the sauce over the crêpes and sprinkle with the grated Parmesan. Bake for 30 minutes, or until the sauce is bubbling and the top is nicely browned. Allow the manicotti to cool for 5 minutes before serving.

Serves 4 generously, plus a little extra because you look skinny

Käsespätzle

MOUNTAIN MAC

TRADITIONAL: *German alpine cheese, such as Adelegger*
SUBSTITUTION: *Roth Grand Cru Surchoix*

This German version of mac and cheese is made with fresh, nutmeg-laced noodles. My first trip to the Bavarian Alps included a memorable version. I was staying with a small family that produced one wheel of cheese a day. At dawn, the husband and wife milked the cows and combined each morning's milk with the previous afternoon's before cooking it in a large copper pot over a wood fire. From this they'd make a single fifty-pound wheel of golden, grassy cheese. One evening, she cooked käsespätzle for us after we'd been hiking in the Alps all day. Her cooking commanded all of my senses: I smelled the onions caramelizing, saw the steam wafting from the pot of boiling water through the chilly evening air, and heard the repetitive whipping of the spätzle batter. She expertly pushed the batter through a screen, dropping little worms of pasta into the boiling water. She grated an obscenely large hunk of cheese—which she'd made with her own hands the previous summer—over the hot spätzle, topped that with the dark brown onions, then grated even more cheese on top, before declaring dinner ready. Everything about that trip was slow—the milking, the cheese making, but especially that endless wait for her käsespätzle. I ate that mac and cheese in four or five minutes, but I've never forgotten it.

6 tablespoons unsalted butter

2 large yellow onions, finely chopped (about 2 cups)

1 bay leaf

3½ cups all-purpose flour

1 teaspoon kosher salt, plus more for salting the pasta water

¼ teaspoon freshly grated nutmeg

4 eggs

1¼ cups milk

8 ounces cheese of choice, shredded (about 2 cups)

½ cup finely chopped flat-leaf parsley

Freshly ground black pepper

Melt 2 tablespoons of the butter in a medium sauté pan over medium heat, then add the onions and bay leaf. Reduce the heat to medium-low and cook, stirring occasionally, until the onions are deeply caramelized, about 50 minutes. Discard the bay leaf and set the onions aside.

(continued)

While the onions cook, bring a large pot of salted water to a boil and make the noodles.

Add the flour, salt, and nutmeg to the bowl of a stand mixer fitted with the whisk attachment and mix to combine. Make a well in the center of the flour mixture and add the eggs and milk.

Attach a dough hook to the mixer and knead on medium-low speed until the dough is soft and quite sticky, about 10 minutes. (The dough should be soft enough that it drips off the tip of your finger after a minute but is still somewhat elastic.) If the dough is too dry, add a splash more milk; if too wet, add a bit more flour. Continue to knead until large air pockets or bubbles appear.

Once the water comes to a full, rolling boil, reduce the heat to keep it at a good simmer. Place a colander with large holes or a cooling rack with a small, square grid over the water. (If you happen to have a spätzle press, now's the time to use it!) Scoop up about ¼ cup or so of the dough with a pastry cutter or a large flexible spatula and push it through the colander, rack, or press, so that small noodles drop into the simmering water to cook. Cook the spätzle until they float to the surface, 2 to 3 minutes. Using a skimmer or spider, remove the cooked spätzle to a separate colander placed over a bowl or in the sink. Repeat this process until all of the dough is cooked. Rinse the cooked spätzle with cool water and run your hands through it to break up any clumps. Drain well. Dump the cooking water and return the pot to stove.

Melt the remaining 4 tablespoons (½ stick) butter in the same pot over medium heat, then add the spätzle and warm it through, 2 to 3 minutes. Stirring constantly, add the shredded cheese and most of the onions, and continue to stir until the cheese is melted. Turn out onto a serving platter and garnish with the remaining onions and the parsley. Season with black pepper and serve immediately.

Serves 4, though they may yodel for more

THE OFFICIAL BEV OF BAVARIA
Beer

In Bavaria the air is clean, the mountain grass is a lush green, and the beer flows as fresh and fast as spring water. The following beers are made in styles typical of Bavaria. I wouldn't think of pairing anything else with käsespätzle.

HEFEWEIZEN

Everything you'd want in a Bavarian hefeweizen (wheat beer) is found in **Weihenstephaner Hefeweissbier**, a golden pour of yeasty brew, with pleasing banana notes and a creamy yet refreshing finish. (What I drank with my first alpine käsespätzle!)

PILSNER

A pilsner named for *Prima!*—a German exclamation of joy—easy-drinking **Victory Brewing Co. Prima Pils** is earthy, herbal, and clean. A weeknight beer for weeknight German mac.

MAIBOCK

Rogue Ales Dead Guy Ale is a maibock-style brew by way of Oregon. A dark, malty, rich brew that mimics the deep, roasted flavors of the käsespätzle's caramelized onions.

RAUCHBIER

A dark rauchbier (smoked beer), **Aecht Schlenkerla Rauchbier Märzen** has sweet dried-fruit notes (think raisins and stewed plums) and a round, full-bodied smokiness. It's especially good at picking up on the nutty flavors and nutmeg in the käsespätzle.

Kugel with Cottage Cheese, Leeks, & Dill

COMFORT CHEESE

Cottage cheese was a favorite of early colonial settlers, who made it at home in their "cottages." I especially love it with warm egg noodles, a habit formed as a kid in my own home and at the homes of Jewish friends, where it was served as kugel. Over the years, I've gussied up the basic concept by adding crème fraîche, leeks melted in butter, and a sizable amount of dill (by far my favorite fresh herb). Lemon zest lends brightness, and a flurry of creamy feta adds salt and soul. My cottage-cheese-and-noodle dish is "good enough for company"—as my grandmother would say—while still satisfying my nostalgic craving.

Kosher salt

8 tablespoons (1 stick) unsalted butter, plus more for greasing the baking dish

4 leeks, trimmed, halved lengthwise, and thinly sliced (about 2 cups)

3 garlic cloves, minced

¼ teaspoon white pepper

12 ounces wide egg noodles

4 eggs, lightly beaten

24 ounces cottage cheese (about 3 cups)

8 ounces crème fraîche, such as Vermont Creamery (1 cup)

1 tablespoon lemon zest

4 ounces feta, crumbled (about ¾ cups)

¾ cup finely chopped fresh dill

Preheat the oven to 350°F. Bring a large pot of salted water to a boil. Butter a 3-quart or 9 x 13-inch baking dish.

In a medium sauté pan over medium heat, melt 2 tablespoons of the butter until foaming. Add the leeks and cook, stirring occasionally, until the leeks are bright green and slightly wilted, about 5 minutes. Stir in 2 more tablespoons of the butter, garlic, and white pepper and continue to cook until the leeks are very soft, another 5 minutes.

(continued)

Once the water is at a full boil, cook the pasta according to the package instructions until just al dente. Melt the remaining 4 tablespoons (½ stick) of butter.

In a large bowl, whisk together the eggs, cottage cheese, crème fraîche, lemon zest, half the feta, and 1 teaspoon of salt in a large bowl. Stir in the melted butter.

When the noodles are ready, drain them and combine them with the cheese mixture. Stir in the dill and pour the mixture into the buttered baking dish. Top with the remaining feta and bake until bubbling and browned on the edges, about 45 minutes. Allow to set and cool for 5 minutes before serving.

Serves 4 as a main or 8 as a side

Mac & Cheese Combinations to Win Friends & Influence People

Sometimes it's fun to mix things up! A custom cheese blend can deepen and improve the flavor of your mac, taking it from good (but predictable) to signature-dish status. Some tips for your bespoke blend:

HONOR THE RELATIONSHIP

Think about how your cheese choices relate to each other. For example, if you're set on including a salty cheese, make sure the cheeses you blend it with aren't salty. Similarly, mild cheeses should blend with cheeses that bring more flavor to the mix.

MAKE IT MELT

Some cheeses melt better than others. Ensure your blend will have that stretch and pull you want by including at least one cheese that is an excellent, surefire, no-worry melter. These ol' reliables should be the dominant cheeses in the blend. Think fontina, young cheddar, Jarlsberg, or Gruyère.

BLENDED FAMILY

Sometimes blending two or three of the "same" cheeses can yield the depth of flavor we expect from mixing it up: mild, young Gouda, a flavored Gouda, and an aged Gouda, for example. Similarly, blending an unflavored cheese into a flavored one can help highlight that flavor without letting it overpower the whole dish.

DOT WITH FRESH CHEESE

Fresh cheeses, such as ricotta and chèvre, don't melt as much as get hot and creamy. What a treat to find little pockets of warm creaminess dotted throughout your mac. Add fresh cheeses to the mac by hand, dotted on top before baking, as opposed to mixing them into the cheese blend.

Cheese, Air, Sex, Magic

THERE'S A SPECIAL PLACE ON MY CHURCH OF CHEESUS ALTAR for air-puffed cheese extravagances, because it's only by magic, alchemy, and the powers vested in cheese that the lightness of a gougère or the dramatic, fragile height of a soufflé is made possible, given their copious amounts of dense dairy.

When cooking with cheese, "lightening things up" can mean adding acidity or spice and it can also mean harnessing the power of hot air. Hot air needs to move (this is the whole idea behind steam power), and "up" is the easiest direction for it to go (being lighter and less dense than colder air and fairly buzzing with the extra heat energy). This phenomenon is called buoyancy, and it's why a popover puffs and a soufflé ascends.

Despite a relatively small number of ingredients in most puffed batter recipes, many cooks lack confidence when it comes to making them, either because they're unsure of technique or they fear that the end result will simply deflate. But air is an easy-to-use, badass ingredient—and it's free! And while it's true that technique is important—oven temperature, ingredient ratios, and timing are all key—once you understand the basic premise of these recipes, they are quite simple to execute and can be easily adapted to any number of cheeses and add-ins. Confidence is key, and if you must, fake it 'til you bake it. With practice, self-assuredness will find you.

I was tempted to call this chapter "Don't Open the Oven!" because that's the cardinal rule when harnessing hot air ("eat immediately" is the other important one).

Classic Cheese Soufflé

THE HIGHER THE PUFF, THE CLOSER TO GOD

TRADITIONAL: *Gruyère*

SUBSTITUTIONS: *alpine or alpine-style cheeses such as Comté, Emmentaler, Uplands Cheese Pleasant Ridge Reserve, or Jasper Hill Farm Alpha Tolman*

A cheese soufflé is always a good bet for entertaining; people love the fleeting height—the anticipatory drama of the inevitable fall of a soufflé—the whiff of nostalgia, and, of course, an airy custard rich with grassy, nutty mountain cheese.

3 tablespoons unsalted butter, plus more for greasing the soufflé dish

1 tablespoon grated Parmigiano Reggiano

3 tablespoons all-purpose flour

1 cup milk

½ teaspoon ground mustard

½ teaspoon white pepper

½ teaspoon kosher salt

5 eggs, yolks and whites separated

4 ounces cheese of choice, shredded (1 cup)

Preheat the oven to 400°F. Butter the bottom and sides of a 1½-quart soufflé dish. Dust the bottom and sides with the Parmigiano Reggiano and set aside.

In a medium saucepan over medium heat, melt the butter to foaming. Add the flour, whisking constantly until the mixture has a nutty aroma and the color of toasted cashews, about 5 minutes. Whisk in the milk and cook, whisking constantly, until the sauce is as thick as drinkable yogurt, about 5 minutes. Remove from the heat, whisk in the ground mustard, white pepper, and salt and cool to lukewarm.

Once the béchamel is cool, whisk in the egg yolks one at a time, mixing thoroughly after each addition. Pour the mixture into a large, clean bowl.

(continued)

In a stand mixer fitted with the whisk attachment or in a separate large bowl, beat the egg whites until very stiff, about 5 minutes. Gently fold one-quarter of the beaten egg whites into the soufflé mixture with a flexible spatula, until just combined (you don't want to deflate the whites, but you don't want large streaks of white, either). Alternating with the cheese, fold one-third of the remaining beaten egg whites into the batter, then one-third of the shredded cheese. Continue until all of the egg whites and cheese have been incorporated. Transfer the batter to the prepared soufflé dish.

Place the dish in the oven and immediately reduce the temperature to 350°F. Bake until the soufflé puffs and is golden brown, 25 to 30 minutes. Serve immediately.

Serves 6 to 8 lucky souls with a bearable lightness of being

SERIOUSLY:

Don't. Open. The Oven.

If you do, your puff will not reach the heights it was meant to, and all your hard work will be squandered at the finish line.

Gougères

REWARD FOR WINE-ING

TRADITIONAL: *Gruyère*

SUBSTITUTIONS: *any alpine or alpine-style cheese or Sottocenere al Tartufo, if you're in the mood for truffles*

The French don't snack much, but when they do, it's on gougères, usually with a glass of white wine. These elegant one-bite wonders can be served hot or at room temperature, but a fresh gougère with a chilled glass of crisp Sancerre or white Bordeaux (see White Wines [& Beers] for Gougères, page 160) is a lesson in contrasts of flavor, texture, and temperature. The savory, softly cloud-like biscuit and bracing, sharp wine prove that opposites attract and collide, deliciously. A firm truffle cheese would be especially decadent here.

½ cup milk

8 tablespoons (1 stick) unsalted butter, cubed

½ teaspoon ground mustard

½ teaspoon kosher salt

1 cup all-purpose flour

4 eggs

5 ounces cheese of choice, shredded (about 1¼ cups)

Preheat the oven to 400°F with racks in the upper and lower third. Line 2 baking sheets with parchment paper or silicone baking mats.

In a medium saucepan over medium heat, bring ½ cup water, the milk, butter, mustard, and salt to a gentle boil. Reduce the heat to medium-low and add the flour, stirring vigorously with a wooden spoon until the mixture looks like mashed potatoes, about 2 minutes.

Cook, stirring constantly, until the dough smells nutty and looks dry around the edges, another 3 minutes. (The bottom of the pan will develop a thin crust of dough during this time, but don't worry, it's to be expected.)

(continued)

Transfer the dough to a stand mixer fitted with the paddle attachment and mix at medium speed until the dough is cool enough to touch, 4 to 5 minutes. Add the eggs, one at a time, incorporating completely before adding the next one. Scrape down the sides of the bowl and mix for 1 more minute.

Mix in the shredded cheese until combined. The dough should be smooth and sticky, like a cheese-dotted cake batter. Place rounded tablespoons of the dough on the prepared baking sheets.

Put the baking sheets in the oven and immediately reduce the oven temperature to 375°F. Bake for 12 minutes, then rotate the pans and switch them between top and bottom racks and bake about 12 more minutes, until the gougères are uniformly golden and look dry. Serve hot, straight from the oven, or cooled to room temperature.

Makes 24 cheesy puffs

White Wines (& Beers) for Gougères

DOMAINE CARNEROS BRUT

Utilize the bubbles in Domaine Carneros Brut (California) to add another layer of airy magic to the gougère experience. Carbonation and acidity help break down the butterfat of the gougère, so that you'll want to keep sipping and snacking.

JOSEPH DROUHIN POUILLY-FUISSÉ CHARDONNAY

If you like traditional pairings, Joseph Drouhin Pouilly-Fuissé Chardonnay (Burgundy, France) is a nutty, medium-bodied wine with the classic characteristics of the appellation: floral, fruity, and fresh.

PAUL BLANCK CLASSIQUE RIESLING

The contrast between the rich puffs and the bright and very dry Paul Blanck Classique Riesling (Alsace, France) will have a sensorial effect similar to enthusiastically nodding your head yes. This pairing goes back and forth, back and forth.

ALLAGASH BREWING COMPANY CONFLUENCE ALE

Allagash Brewing Company Confluence Ale is an approachable American sour with a yeasty, bready vibe. Its relatively mild sourness plays a nice duet with the gougères' warm, airy, and slightly eggy core.

BROUWERIJ VERHAEGHE DUCHESSE DE BOURGOGNE

In a hearty, worthy pairing, the subtle sweetness of Brouwerij Verhaeghe Duchesse de Bourgogne (Belgium) sour ale mimics the sweetness that blooms in Gruyère during baking.

Popover Country

Let other recipes in the book inspire all-new popover variations:

CHÈVRE & GUAVA

The recipe inspiring this combo calls for queso de freir, but that's not the right fit for a popover because it's a grilling and frying cheese. Instead, opt for a chèvre, which shares an equally straightforward vibe and also pairs well with guava paste. After filling the muffin cups with batter, drop a dollop of chèvre and a small pat of guava paste into each cup and bake. *(see page 37)*

KOPANISTI

After filling the muffin cups with batter, sprinkle a teaspoon of finely crumbled Greek feta and a pinch of chopped dill into each cup and bake. Drizzle the finished popovers with Greek honey if you're looking to skew sweet, or serve with a side of olive tapenade for more savory schmearing. *(see Baked Feta with Pickled Peppers & Dill, page 46)*

FRENCH ONION

Make the French Onion Soup (see page 105). Make a batch of plain Popovers (see page 164). Ladle the soup into individual crocks. Place a popover in the crock, on top of the soup. Drape the crock with Gruyère and broil until the cheese melts, bubbles, and browns.

POUTINE

Make the Lazy Gravy (see page 94) or reheat leftover gravy. Place 2 hot, fresh-from-the-oven popovers in a shallow bowl and sprinkle with 5 or 6 room temperature cheese curds. Pour the hot gravy over the popovers and curds and serve immediately.

Smoked Gouda & Bacon Dutch Baby

UP IN SMOKE

TRUSTED BRANDS: *Maple Leaf, Marieke*

A Dutch baby is a buttery little puff of tender pancake made from a thin batter that rises and crisps around the edges as it bakes. It's equally good savory or sweet, and frankly can be a platform for both at the same time. The base recipe rewards experimentation and variation, but keep in mind that solid add-ins, such as fruits and vegetables or meat, should be mixed into the batter before it goes in the pan—simply piling them on top of the raw batter will hinder the all-important rise. Other melting cheeses, such as Gruyère or cheddar, may be shredded over the risen baby before returning it to the oven.

2 pieces thick-cut bacon, chopped

½ cup all-purpose flour

½ cup milk

3 eggs

¼ teaspoon kosher salt

2 tablespoons unsalted butter, melted and cooled slightly

2 ounces smoked Gouda, shredded (about ⅓ cup)

1 tablespoon finely chopped chives

Maple syrup, for finishing (optional)

Preheat the oven to 425°F.

Cook the bacon in a 10-inch cast-iron pan over medium heat until crisp and the fat has rendered, about 6 minutes. Using a slotted spoon, transfer the bacon to paper towels to drain. Pour the fat into a small bowl and set it aside. Wipe out the hot pan with a wad of paper towels and place the pan in the oven to preheat.

In a food processor, add the flour, milk, eggs, and salt and process for 2 minutes. Drizzle in the melted butter with the processor running. Keep the batter in the bowl of the food processor and place it in the refrigerator to rest for 10 minutes.

(continued)

After the batter has rested, remove the cast-iron pan from the oven and pour in the reserved bacon fat, swirling it to coat. Pour the batter into the pan, return it to the oven, and bake for 18 minutes, until puffed and just golden brown on top.

Remove the Dutch baby from the oven, sprinkle it with the cooked bacon and the shredded cheese, and return it to the oven until the cheese is melted, another 2 to 3 minutes. Garnish with the chives and serve immediately. A wee drizzle of maple syrup never hurt anyone.

Serves 2 as a wake and bake

Pecorino Popover

A popover is essentially a smaller Dutch baby (same ingredients and process for both), made in a muffin or popover pan. Across the pond it's called Yorkshire pudding, and served with gravy to dramatic effect.

To the base recipe for the Dutch baby, add ½ cup finely grated Pecorino and bake in a preheated and greased muffin or popover pan, instead of a cast-iron pan.

Fill each cup just shy of halfway so the popovers have room to rise.

Bake at 400°F for 10 minutes, then reduce the oven to 350°F and continue to bake until puffed and lightly golden, about 7 more minutes, for a total cooking time of about 17 minutes.

Makes 12

Pão de Queijo

(GLUTEN-FREE) BRAZILIAN CHEESE BREAD

RECOMMENDED: *young Manchego, young cheddar, mozzarella*

These brilliantly airy Brazilian cheese rolls—similar to gougères—are naturally gluten-free because they're made from tapioca flour, a staple of Brazilian cooking found in most supermarkets with Latin foods sections. The tapioca ensures a crisp outer crust that gives way to a pleasing, chewy bite as you eat closer to the center. They're best served fresh out of the oven, though at room temperature they're still tasty (and a bit chewier).

1 cup whole milk	2½ cups tapioca flour
½ cup canola oil	2 eggs
½ teaspoon kosher salt	6 ounces cheese of choice, shredded (about 1½ cups)

Preheat the oven to 425°F. Arrange two racks in the upper and lower thirds of the oven. Line 2 baking sheets with parchment paper or silicone baking mats.

In a medium saucepan over medium heat, bring the milk, oil, and salt to a gentle boil, removing the pan from the heat as soon as bubbles appear on the surface. Add the tapioca flour, stirring until incorporated and the dough looks thick and gummy. Transfer the dough to a stand mixer fitted with the paddle attachment and mix at medium speed until just cool enough to touch, 4 to 5 minutes.

Add the eggs, one at a time, completely incorporating the first egg before adding the second. Scrape down the sides of the bowl and mix for 1 more minute. The dough will be sticky, oily, a little lumpy, and look like cookie dough. (This is okay! You're on the right track.) Add the cheese and mix until incorporated, about 2 minutes.

Dip your fingers in a bowl of water and pinch off 1 tablespoon of the dough, form it into a ball (you don't need to be precise here), and place it on a baking sheet. Repeat with the remaining dough, dividing the balls evenly between the 2 prepared baking sheets.

Place the baking sheets in the oven and immediately reduce the oven temperature to 350°F. Bake for 8 minutes, then rotate the pans and switch them between the top and bottom racks. Bake for another 20 minutes, until the pãos are golden on the bottom edges and look dry. Cool on a rack for 5 minutes before serving.

Makes 24 gluten-free cheesy puffs

Raclette's Get It On

LIKE MANY FOOD-OBSESSED FOLK, I'VE SPENT AN INORDINATE amount of time thinking about what my last meal would be (if I were lucky enough to be able to choose). Obviously it would include cheese, and I'm declaring raclette as my final answer—the cheese and the experience.

Raclette is a semi-firm to firm brine-washed cow's milk cheese originally from the French and Swiss Alps. It derives its name from the French verb *racler*, "to scrape," and has a dense, supple, golden paste that shares flavor characteristics with fellow alpine cheeses like Gruyère and Comté. Its flavors range from mild and slightly nutty with grassy notes to full-bodied with oniony, meaty, and brothy tones, dependent on producer and production (how long it's washed and aged). Raclette's slightly sticky rind is meant to be eaten.

Traditionally, these fifteen-pound wheels of cheese were halved or quartered and their exposed paste heated fireside. The melted cheese was then scraped onto bread, potatoes, pickles, and anything else within reach—somewhat like a reverse fondue, but instead of dunking bits of this and that into hot cheese one by one, everything on the plate is decadently enrobed in glorious, gluttonous hot cheese heaven.

In the United States, there are many producers of raclette-style cheese (see American Raclette, page 175). Similar to their European muse, American raclette cheeses are made from cow's milk, with an orangey-pink washed rind and a paste of varying alpine-esque flavor profiles. Most cheese shops carry either a Swiss or French raclette (French is much more common, as it tends to be more wallet friendly) and at least one American raclette. Don't be afraid to buy a wedge of each and serve them side by side for a cheesy international joint summit.

One of the many reasons I'm hot for raclette is that it's essentially customizable cheese porn with an unlimited number of combinations—kind of like the *Kama Sutra* of cheese. You could eat an entire raclette meal and never have the same bite twice. I particularly enjoy sharing a new combination discovery (one or two accompaniments + hot cheese) with friends during the meal. Raclette is both a treasure hunt for the finest bite and the gold at the end of the quest.

A simple format for building a raclette meal is to select a cheese for melting, a starch to bulk up the meal, some veggies and/or meats for flavor and nutritional balance, a few pickled or brined bites to offset the richness of the cheese, and a fruit or two for a little something sweet. Go as low-effort or as elaborate as you want here, purchasing your accompaniments or cooking them on your own.

Raclette is really just a dish featuring cheese melted on top of other foods, so it's vital to focus on quality when choosing those foods. Select only the highest-quality breads, vegetables, and meats you have access to, and slice and serve them with care (for successful melting, cut your cheese into approximately ⅓-inch slices) and flair (remember, we eat with our eyes as much as our mouths). For a weeknight meal, consider two or three accompaniments. For an all-out affair, go as elaborate as you dare—the more tasty the nibbles, the more exciting the combinations your guests will discover.

I've placed raclette at the end of this book (and as my imagined last meal) because it creates camaraderie through melted cheese, and beyond the deliciousness of melted cheese, that's what makes it special. We all know the secret ingredient to a great meal is who you share it with. So gather your people. It's time for hot cheese.

There's More Than One Way to Raclette

There are four basic categories of raclette machines for home use, from pans that use open flame to melt a slice of cheese to electric machines that melt a half wheel. The raclette machines photographed here are all made by Boska, a family-run Dutch manufacturer of cheese tools since 1896.

CANDLE-POWERED RACLETTE PANS

These self-contained raclette pans sit above a candle-powered base that melts one slice of cheese at a time. They're a good choice if you're not all in on the raclette lifestyle (yet), as you can purchase them individually for a reasonable $20 to $25. (See Melt the Moon, page 180, and Italian Feast, page 183)

BBQ RACLETTE PANS

A similar concept to the candle-powered pans, except powered by your outdoor grill. If you're concerned that raclette is a winter food, don't sweat it. Hot cheese has no season. A fairly low-cost purchase at $20 to $25.

ELECTRIC RACLETTE MACHINES

If you're ready to commit to raclette as a go-to for meals or entertaining, you may be ready for an electric raclette machine. These machines typically hold six to eight individual pans that are heated above an electric coil. One of the perks—besides the capacity to melt several individual servings at once—is a heated tray or griddle to keep accompaniments warm. You get what you pay for with these machines, which run from $50 to $150, so invest in quality if you decide to take the plunge.

ELECTRIC HALF- AND QUARTER-WHEEL HEAT LAMPS

These machines are for the fully committed raclette lover ready to host hot cheese parties. They require more attention than the machines that rely on individual pans for melt: someone will need to melt and scrape the cheese from a quarter wheel (see American Ingenuity, page 179) or half-wheel (see French Connection, page 176). Prices range from $60 to $450.

Raclette It All

Practically any good melting cheese can be used for raclette. Alpine and washed-rind cheeses are of particular note, as they most closely deliver on the classic raclette flavor profile. Raclette is all about mixing and matching, so don't be afraid to experiment with more accessible or affordable cheeses or to serve something from the supermarket next to a more specialized (and pricier) cheese.

ALPINE AND ALPINE-STYLE

Emmental, Gruyère, Jarlsberg

WASHED-RIND

Fontina Valle d'Aosta, Meadow Creek Dairy Grayson, Taleggio

SUPERMARKET FAVES

Fontal, Havarti, Monterey Jack

WILD CARDS

Brie, mozzarella, young Gouda

American Raclette

In Europe the right to name a cheese raclette is protected by laws set by individual countries and within the European Union that define strict guidelines about how and where some cheeses are produced. Unencumbered by law or tradition, American cheese makers also produce their own versions, to delicious result.

EAST HILL CREAMERY UNDERPASS

East Hill Creamery Underpass from New York is a young raclette-style cheese that's mild, smooth, and milky.

LEELANAU CHEESE RACLETTE

Leelanau Cheese Raclette from Michigan is made by a Swiss-trained cheese maker, who produces several styles of award-winning raclette, including plain and black truffle.

ROTH ROASTED GARLIC RACLETTE

Roth Roasted Garlic Raclette from Wisconsin is one of a line of several accessible, big-brand raclettes, including other flavored options like Five Peppercorn and Mediterranean, with olives and sun-dried tomatoes.

YELLOW DOOR CREAMERY VALIS

Yellow Door Creamery Valis from New Jersey is fruity and übermelty.

French Connection

Consider this accessible, elegant menu an introduction to how the French do raclette. It's a sound road map for a maiden voyage, since all of the accompaniments are purchased and offer familiar flavors and a double dose of carbs (bread and potatoes, you complete me).

THE CHEESE: *French Raclette*

French raclette is firm and quite fruity, with a pleasing salinity thanks to its brine-washed rind. It's generally the most affordable raclette option, and available at more cheese counters than Swiss raclette (though, of course, feel free to tag in Swiss, if you'd like).

THE STARCH: *Bien Cuit Baguette and Boiled Baby Potatoes*

Choose the freshest, best-quality baguette you can find (I buy mine from Bien Cuit Bakery in Brooklyn), and boil the potatoes in liberally salted water. Toss a bay leaf in the boil to lend a nice herbal note to the potatoes.

THE PICKLE AND CURE: *Cornichon and Losada Olives*

Pair crisp, tart, clove-spiked cornichons—a classic French pickle made from mini gherkin cucumbers—with olives from Losada, a family-run producer of traditional Spanish and heirloom olives based in Seville, Spain. Pictured are blush-colored Cornicabra, a rich, intensely flavored olive from Central Spain, which is named for a goat's horns; Empeltre, a soft black olive from Aragon that's fruity and creamy; and Gordal a large, pulpy green table olive from Seville.

THE (OTHER) PROTEIN: *Charlito's Cocina Trufa Seca*

Charlito's Cocina makes small-batch, dry-cured sausages from heritage breed pork. Their Trufa Seca, made with black truffles and sea salt, is packed with minerally, umami-driven, pork-tastic flavor.

THE FRUIT: *Fresh Grapes and Raisins*

Go for a variety of grapes, for flavor and color variation. If you can find them, raisins on the vine make for a beautiful presentation.

American Ingenuity

This all-American menu follows the raclette format laid out in the chapter opening, but with an American twist (you probably won't see tater tots at many French or Swiss raclette meals). There's a bit more cooking here than in the French menu, but it's starter level and foolproof: roast some carrots, griddle some sausages, and you're good to go.

THE CHEESE: *Spring Brook Farm Reading*

Vermont's Spring Brook Farm makes superlative cheese for a cause: it's part of a program that teaches urban kids about farming and cheese making. Reading is faithful to the raclette style, with a firm, pleasingly salty paste, but its deep nutty and fruit-driven notes make it a more full-bodied choice than its French counterpart.

THE STARCH: *Tater Tots*

Everybody. Loves. Tater tots. What more can I say besides bake them until they're extracrispy? Soggy tots are a flop.

THE PICKLE: *Preservation & Co. Hickory Brussels Sprouts*

These distinctive pickles from California take inspiration from the classic combination of brussels sprouts and bacon (though they're meat-free). Apple cider vinegar, liquid hickory smoke, and a blend of dried peppers and aromatic seeds make this unique pickle a flavorful, tangy base for hot cheese.

THE (OTHER) PROTEIN: *Grilled Fresh Sausages*

I like uniquely seasoned sausages for raclette: they layer in some surprising flavors. The sausages pictured here are Chicken Kale Pesto and Mexican Red Chorizo from Brooklyn-based Foster Sundry, my favorite cheese shop and butchery in New York City.

THE VEG: *Roasted Carrots*

Olive oil, salt, pepper, and a hot oven are all you need to properly roast carrots. Be mindful not to overcook them though—a limpid carrot is a big bummer. Twelve or so minutes is usually all they need.

THE FRUIT: *Fresh and Dried Apples*

If you want to slice your apples ahead of time, float them in some lemon water so they don't brown and drain them on paper towels before serving.

Melt the Moon

This raclette is built around a Gouda-inspired goat's milk cheese—for flavor and fun, and for folks who have a hard time digesting cow's milk cheeses. Russophile accompaniments featuring beets, dill, and brown bread keep the race to the moon relevant.

THE CHEESE: *Cypress Grove Midnight Moon*

I think of Midnight Moon as cheese candy because it's full of up-front nutty, caramel, and sweet brown butter notes. Since goat's milk cheeses don't generally melt as smoothly as cow's milk cheeses do, consider slicing your Moon a tad more thinly than you would raclette, to give it a better shot at going full-on gooey.

THE STARCH: *Bien Cuit Rye Ficelle and Dill Pickle Potato Chips*

What would a Russian-inspired meal be without some brown bread, potatoes, and dill flavor? Not much.

THE PICKLE: *Rick's Picks Phat Beets*

These aromatic pickled beets from New York City–based Rick's Picks are laced with ginger, rosemary, and lemon, for a perky, earthy bite.

THE (OTHER) PROTEIN: *Hard-Boiled Chicken and Quail Eggs*

The only thing better than a perfectly hard-boiled egg is two varieties of them, which make them friendlier for combining with other ingredients. Don't forget to season liberally with salt and pepper.

THE VEG: *Roasted Mushrooms*

Larger mushroom varieties are key here, for flavor and ease of service. Roast them whole or in larger portions, to provide optimal surface area for draping in cheese.

THE FRUIT: *Fresh Pears*

If you want to slice your pears ahead of time, float them in some lemon water so they don't brown and drain them on paper towels before serving.

Italian Feast

This menu is raclette as a riot of antipasti, featuring a unique Italian cheese made from rich, custardy buffalo's milk. Aromatic pickles help cut through the richness of the rest of the accompaniments.

THE CHEESE: *Quadrello di Bufala*

Quadrello di Bufala is a Taleggio-style buffalo's milk cheese from Lombardy, Italy, with a semi-soft paste encased in a ruddy washed rind. It's milky and sweet, with notes of hay and freshly turned soil.

THE STARCH: *Roasted Sweet Potatoes and Bien Cuit Pugliese*

Roasted sweet potatoes draw out the natural sweetness of buffalo's milk, and hearty potato bread provides another platform for sopping up some cheese.

THE PICKLE: *Olympia Provisions Pickled Celery and Pickled Cocktail Onions*

Based in Portland, Oregon, Olympia Provisions is known for its charcuterie, but its pickles are worth a closer look. The company works with local farms to produce its pickles in season, which is apparent from their clean, compact flavors. Pickled onions are a traditional pairing with raclette.

THE (OTHER) PROTEIN: *Prosciutto di Parma*

Prosciutto di Parma is a dry-cured ham made in and around the countryside of Parma, in north-central Italy. This buttery, sweet ham pairs especially well with the milky melt of Quadrello di Bufala.

THE VEG: *Grilled Peppers and Zucchini*

Grill them simply, either on a grill or in a grill pan, with olive oil, salt, and pepper.

THE FRUIT: *Quince and Apple Pear Mostarda*

Yes, technically pear mostarda isn't a fruit, but it's so delightfully packed with juicy pears that I'm okay stretching the format of the menu here. This traditional Italian condiment, by way of Madison, Wisconsin, answers the richness of Quadrello di Bufala with sweet, tart, and aromatic notes, and the pears are cut coarsely, so they don't get lost texturally when slathered on bread and draped in silken cheese.

Index

(Page references in *italic* refer to illustrations.)

acid-set cheeses, 11
Aligot, 120, *121*
American Ingenuity raclette menu, *178*, 179
Asian flavors, in Bread Cheese with Tamari,
    Maple, & Thai Chiles, *34*, 35

beef:
    in Pljeskavica, *92*, 93
    steaks, in Francesinha, 94–96, *95*
beers:
    Bavarian, 147
    for gougères, 160
BelGioiso Kasseri, 40
bloomy-rind cheeses, for baked dips, 56
blue cheese(s), 13
    Colcannon Stew with Bacon &, 108–10, *109*
    cooking with, 110
    Dip, Buffalo Cheese Curds with, 72
    Sauce, 25, 28, *29*, 129
Brazilian flavors, in Pão de Queijo, *166*, 167
bread:
    bowl, French Onion Soup in, *104*, 105–6
    Pão de Queijo, *166*, 167
Bread Cheese with Tamari, Maple, & Thai
    Chiles, *34*, 35
Brie Kataifi, Baked, with Honey, *54*, 55
Broccoli Cheddar Soup, 111–12, *113*
Buck Rabbit, 24
BuffArepa, *88*, 89–90
burgers:
    Rarebit, 24
    Stuffed (Pljeskavica), *92*, 93
burrata:
Fried, with Roasted Tomatoes, 62–64, *63*
Mac & Cheese, *138*, 139
butter, clarified, 87

cabbage, in Colcannon Stew with Bacon & Blue
    Cheese, 108–10, *109*
canola oil, 80

cast-iron cookware, 14, 41
cheddar:
    Broccoli Soup, 111–12, *113*
    Goat Cheese Queso Fundido, 58, 59
    Grilled Cheese, *84*, 85–87, 91
    Pão de Queijo, *166*, 167
    Rarebit Sauce, 22–24, *23*, 25, 129
cheese curds:
    Buffalo, with Blue Cheese Dip, 72
    Fried, 70–73, *71*
    Poutine with Lazy Gravy, *130*, 131
    reliable producers of, 81
cheese-making process, 11
cheese-plate cheeses, 11–12
chèvre, 11, 117
    Fried, *66*, 67–69
    popovers with guava &, 161
Chips, Pita and Flatbread, 49
Chorizo, Egg, & Cheese Baked Potato,
    126–28, *127*
clarified butter, 87
Colcannon Stew with Bacon & Blue Cheese,
    108–10, *109*
cooking equipment, 14–15, 41
cooking vs. cheese-plate cheeses, 11–12
Corn, Potato, & Cheese Soup, 114–16, *115*
cottage cheese, 117
    Kugel with Leeks, Dill &, 148–50, *149*
Cowgirl Mt Tam, 56
cream cheese, stabilizing cheese sauces
    with, 17
Cypress Grove Midnight Moon, in Melt
    the Moon raclette menu, 180, *181*

dips, baked, 42–58
    bloomy-rind cheeses for, 56
    Brie Kataifi with Honey, *54*, 55
    Feta with Pickled Peppers & Dill, 46, *47*
    Goat Cheese Queso Fundido, 58, *59*
    Pita and Flatbread Chips for, 49

Pumpkin Fondue, 50–53, *51*
Ricotta with Fresh Herbs, *44*, 45
dips, spoon cheeses for, 57
Dutch Baby, Smoked Gouda & Bacon, 162–64, *163*

East Hill Creamery Underpass, 175
egg(s):
Chorizo, & Cheese Baked Potato, 126–28, *127*
Little Dutch, *74*, 75–76

farmer cheese, 117
feta:
Baked, with Pickled Peppers & Dill, 46, *47*
Pljeskavica, *92*, 93
popover variation (kopanisti flavors), 161
produced outside of Greece, 48
finishing cheeses, 14, 125
Flambéed Halloumi with Preserved Lemon & Basil, 32, *33*
Flatbread Chips, 49
fondue:
Pumpkin, Baked, 50–53, *51*
Swiss, 21, 25
fonduta, 25
Truffle, 27, 129
fontina:
for fondue, 53
for grilled cheese, 91
Truffle Fonduta, 27, 129
Francesinha, 94–96, *95*
French Connection raclette menu, 176, *177*
French Onion Soup, *104*, 105–6
popover variation, 161
fresh cheeses, 117
Frico (lacy cheese crackers), 135
Frico (skillet cake), 132–34, *133*
fried cheeses, 60–81
Burrata with Roasted Tomatoes, 62–64, *63*
Cheese Curds, 70–73, *71*
Chèvre, *66*, 67–69
Little Dutch Eggs, *74*, 75–76
Malakoff, 78, *79*
Friend in Cheeses Jam Co., 58
frying oils, 80

Georgian flavors, in Khachipuri, 98–101, *99*
goat cheese:
Cypress Grove Midnight Moon, in Melt the Moon raclette menu, 180, *181*
Queso Fundido, 58, *59*
see also chèvre
Gouda:
for fondue, 53
Little Dutch Eggs, *74*, 75–76
Smoked, & Bacon Dutch Baby, 162–64, *163*
smoked, for grilled cheese, 91
Gougères, 157–60, *159*
Gratin, Potato, with Pancetta & Leeks, *122*, 123–24
Greek flavors:
Baked Brie Kataifi with Honey, *54*, 55
Baked Feta with Pickled Peppers & Dill, 46, *47*
grilled cheese, 83–91
American-Style, *84*, 85–87
BuffArepa, *88*, 89–90
custom cheese blends for, 91
how-to rules for, 86–87
inspired combinations for, 97
grilling cheeses, 40
Gruyère:
Cheese Soufflé, Classic, *154*, 155–56
French Onion Soup, *104*, 105–6, 161
Gougères, 157–60, *159*
for grilled cheese, 86, 91
Malakoff, 78, *79*
Mornay Sauce, 18, *19*, 129
Swiss Fondue, 21, 25
guava:
Paste, Queso de Freir with Oregano Oil &, *36*, 37
popovers with chèvre &, 161

Halloumi Flambé with Preserved Lemon & Basil, 32, *33*
ham, in Francesinha, 94–96, *95*
harissa, New York Shuk brand, 73

Indian flavors, in Paneer in Minted Pea Sauce, 38, *39*
Italian Feast raclette menu, *182*, 183

Italian flavors:
  Frico (lacy cheese crackers), 135
  Frico (skillet cake), 132–34, *133*
  Truffle Fonduta, 27, 129

Jasper Hill Farm:
  Harbison, 57
  Moses Sleeper, 56

Käsespätzle, 144–47
Kasseri, BelGioioso, 40
Kataifi, Baked Brie, with Honey, *54*, 55
Khachipuri, 98–101, *99*
kopanisti, 46, 161
Kugel with Cottage Cheese, Leeks, & Dill,
    148–50, *149*

lamb, in Pljeskavica, *92*, 93
Latin American flavors:
  Goat Cheese Queso Fundido, 58, *59*
  Pão de Queijo, *166*, 167
  Potato, Cheese, & Corn Soup, 114–16, *115*
  Queso de Freir with Guava Paste & Oregano
    Oil, *36*, 37
Lazy Gravy, 48–50, *49*
  popover variation, 161, 164
  Poutine with, *130*, 131
Leelanau Cheese Raclette, 175
linguiça sausage, in Francesinha, 94–96, *95*
Little Dutch Eggs, *74*, 75–76

mac & cheese:
  Burrata, *138*, 139
  custom cheese blends for, 151
  see also pasta and noodles
Malakoff, 78, *79*
Manchego, in Pão de Queijo, *166*, 167
Manicotti 4G, Cheese, 140–43
masarepa, in BuffArepa, *88*, 89–90
mascarpone, Chorizo, Egg, & Cheese Baked
    Potato, 126–28, *127*
Melt the Moon raclette menu, 180, *181*
mixed-milk cheeses, for fondue, 53
Monterey Jack:
  Grilled Cheese, *84*, 85–87, 91
  Potato, Cheese, & Corn Soup, 114–16, *115*
Mornay Sauce, 18, *19*, 129

Mt. Townsend Creamery Cirrus, 56
mozzarella:
  Aligot, 120, *121*
  BuffArepa, *88*, 89–90
  Khachipuri, 98–101, *99*
  Pão de Queijo, *166*, 167

Narragansett Creamery Grilling Cheese, 40
New York Shuk Harissa with Preserved Lemon,
    73
noodles, *see* pasta and noodles

oils, frying, 80
Onion Soup, French, *104*, 105–6
  popover variation, 161

Paneer in Minted Pea Sauce, 38, *39*
Pão de Queijo, *166*, 167
Parsley Sauce, Quick, 68
pasta and noodles, 136–51
  Burrata Mac & Cheese, *138*, 139
  Cheese Manicotti 4G, 140–43
  Käsespätzle, 144–47
  Kugel with Cottage Cheese, Leeks, & Dill,
    148–50, *149*
pastry raft, in Khachipuri, 98–101, *99*
peanut oil, 80
Pea Sauce, Minted, Paneer in, 38, *39*
Pecorino Popover, 164, *165*
Pita Chips, 49
Pleasant Ridge Rush Creek Reserve, 57
Pljeskavica, *92*, 93
popovers:
  Pecorino, 164, *165*
  variations, 161
Portuguese flavors, in Francesinha, 94–96, *95*
potato(es), 118–34
  Aligot, 120, *121*
  baked, bar, 129
  baked, under Rarebit Sauce, 24, 129
  Cheese, & Corn Soup, 114–16, *115*
  Chorizo, Egg, & Cheese Baked, 126–28,
    127
  Colcannon Stew with Bacon & Blue Cheese,
    108–10, *109*
  Frico, 132–34, *133*
Gratin with Pancetta & Leeks, *122*, 123–24
  Poutine with Lazy Gravy, *130*, 131

Poutine with Lazy Gravy, *130*, 131
    popover variation, 161, 164
provoleta, 40
provolone, in Francesinha, 94–96, *95*
puffs:
    Gougères, 157–60, *159*
    Pão de Queijo, *166*, 167
Pumpkin Fondue, Baked, 50–53, *51*

Quadrella di Bufala, in Italian Feast raclette
    menu, *182*, 183
Quebec flavors, in Poutine with Lazy Gravy, *130*,
    131
Queso de Freir with Guava Paste & Oregano Oil,
    36, 37
queso fresco, in Potato, Cheese, & Corn Soup,
    114–16, *115*
Queso Fundido, Goat Cheese, 58, *59*

Raclette (cheese), 169, 175
raclette (meal format), 168–83, *171*, *172*
    American Ingenuity, *178*, 179
    cheeses for, 174, 175
    French Connection, 176, *177*
    Italian Feast, *182*, 183
    machines for, 173
    Melt the Moon, 180, *181*
Rarebit Sauce, 22–24, *23*, 25, 129
rennet-set cheeses, 11
ricotta, 11, 117
    Baked, with Fresh Herbs, *44*, 45
    Cheese Manicotti 4G, 140–43
Roth Roasted Garlic Raclette, 175

salads, seasonal, with Fried Chèvre, 69
salt, 15
sandwiches and "sandwhatevers," 82–101
    Francesinha, 94–96, *95*
    Khachipuri, 98–101, *99*
    Pljeskavica, *92*, 93
    see also grilled cheese
sauces, 16–28
    Blue Cheese, 25, 28, *29*, 129
    foods to serve with, 25
    Mornay, 18, *19*, 129
    Parsley, Quick, 68
    Rarebit, 22–24, *23*, 25, 129
    stabilizing with cream cheese, 17

Swiss Fondue, 21, 25
    Tomato, for Cheese Manicotti 4G, 140, 142
    Truffle Fonduta, 27, 129
science of hot cheese, 10–11
seasoning, adjusting, 15
Soufflé, Classic Cheese, *154*, 155–56
soups, 102–16
    Broccoli Cheddar, 111–12, *113*
    making stock for, 107
    Onion, French, *104*, 105–6, 161
    Potato, Cheese, & Corn, 114–16, *115*
spoon cheeses, baking, 57
Spring Brook Farm Reading, in American
    Ingenuity raclette menu, *178*, 179
stock, making, 107
supermarket cheeses, 13
Sweet Grass Dairy Green Hill, 56
Swiss Fondue, 21, 25

Taleggio:
    Italian Feast raclette menu, *182*, 183
    Potato Gratin with Pancetta & Leeks, *122*,
    123–24
Thanksgiving Francesinha, 96
tomato(es):
    Roasted, Fried Burrata with, 62–64, *63*
    Sauce, for Cheese Manicotti 4G, 140, 142
Truffle Fonduta, 27, 129
turkey, in Thanksgiving Francesinha, 96

vegetable oil, 80
Vermont Creamery St. Albans, 57

Welsh Rarebit, 24
wines:
    red, for Khachipuri, 101
    white, for gougères, 160
    white, in Swiss Fondue, 21, 25

Yanni Grilling Cheese, 40
Yellow Door Creamery Valis, 175
Yugoslav flavors, in Pljeskavica, *92*, 93

Sources

The melt, stretch, and sizzle of hot cheese compel us toward fellowship through feasting, and beautiful wares also make our melting moments memorable. The following artists, artisans, and makers helped shape the images in this book into an unforgettable feast:

Pages 20, 26, 159, 166: Model: Marsha Larose / Parts Models, partsmodels.com; Hair & Makeup: Sacha Harford / Ray Brown Productions, raybrownpro.com

Pages 23, 36: Neon design by John J. Custer, johnjcuster.com

Pages 39, 51, 130: Ceramics by Sabri Ben-Achur, thesabritree.com

Page 54: Cheesus sculpture by Brenda E. Gress, etsy.com/shop/OhMyGodByBrenda

Pages 33, 59, 99, 122, 133, 138, 141, 163: Cast-iron by Lodge, lodgemfg.com

Pages 66, 184–85: Cake stands by Fishs Eddy, fishseddy.com

Page 92: Olive wood wares by Marcelli Formaggi, marcelliformaggi.com; oak table cheese grater by Boska, boska.com

Pages 99, 165: Model: Renee Levine; Hair & Makeup: Sacha Harford / Ray Brown Productions, raybrownpro.com

Pages 163, 172, 177: Ceramics by Josephine Heilpern, recreationcentershop.com

Pages 171, 172, 177, 178, 181, 182: Raclette equipment by Boska, boska.com

Pages 172, 177, 178: Cheese knives by Bharbjt, bharbjt.com

All of the recommended cheeses can be found in supermarkets, specialty cheese shops, or online. Accompaniments, such as jams and chutneys, can be found online or in specialty shops.

Acknowledgments

Thanks to editor Jono Jarrett, photographer Noah Fecks, food stylist Victoria Granof, assistant food stylist Krystal Rack, prop stylist Christopher Spaulding, and Kristin Stangl for additional food styling. Thanks to Lynne Yeamans for layout and design.

Thanks to my agents Kari Stuart and Zoe Sandler at ICM Partners for the above and beyond.

Thanks to Kat Kinsman for being both a champion and a hero.

All of the breads in this book are the work of Brooklyn's Bien Cuit Bakery. Thank you Zachary Golper and Kate Wheatcroft for the bread, support, and friendship.

Thanks to Aaron Foster for graciously allowing us to take pictures at Foster Sundry, your beautiful shop in Bushwick, Brooklyn.

Thanks to the producers and brands who contributed to this book: Aceitunas Losada/Amy Thompson, Beehive Cheese/Pat Ford & Amy Thompson, BelGioioso/Francesca Elfner & Jamie Wichlacz, Boska/Roelien Weenink & Steve Agostinho, La Oveja Negra Manchego/ Raymond Hook, Lodge Cast Iron/Ted Nelson (Gumbo Marketing), Marcelli Formaggi/Andy Marcelli, Marin French Cheese/Susan Wheaton, Preservation and Co./Jason Poole, Quince & Apple/Matt Stoner Fehsenfeld, and Rick's Pick's/Rick Field.

Special thanks to Meredith Reitman, Alexa Weitzman, Cynthea Kimmelman Devries, Rachel Zell, Gabriella Weiss, Randi Greenberg, Elena Santogade, and Liz Thorpe for holding my hand throughout. Thank you to Renee Levine for graciously modeling. Thank you to Aleph Bet Academy for caregiving.

And, finally, the biggest, deepest, most heartfelt thank you to Hristo Zisovski, for everything.

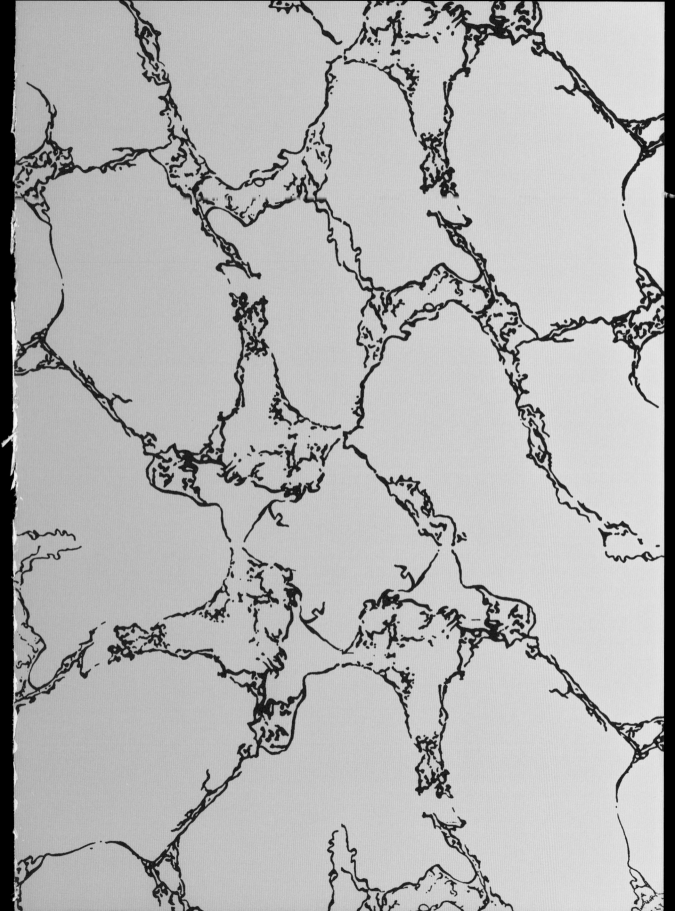

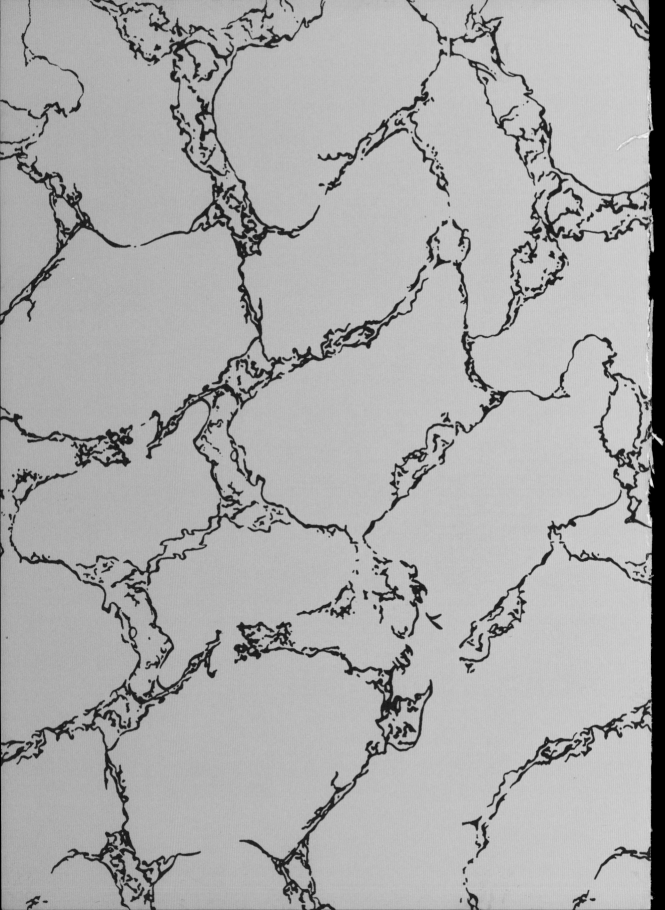